ROCK BENEATH THE SAND

NUMBER FIVE

Sam Rayburn Series on Rural Life

Sponsored by Texas A&M University-Commerce

James A. Grimshaw, Jr., General Editor

TEXAS A&M UNIVERSITY PRESS COLLEGE STATION

ROCK BENEATH THE SAND

COUNTRY CHURCHES IN TEXAS

Photographs by Clark G. Baker

Text by Lois E. Myers & Rebecca Sharpless

Copyright © 2003
by Clark G. Baker, Lois E. Myers, and Rebecca Sharpless
Photographs © 2003 by Clark G. Baker
Printed in China by
Sun Fung Offset Binding Co. Lts.
All rights reserved.
First edition

The paper used in this book
meets the minimum requirements
of the American National Standard for Permanence
of Paper for Printed Library Materials, z39.48-1984.
Binding materials have been chosen for durability.

Library of Congress Cataloging-in-Publication Data

Myers, Lois E., 1946–
        Rock beneath the sand : country churches in Texas / photographs by Clark G. Baker ;
text by Lois E. Myers and Rebecca Sharpless.—1st ed.
                p. cm.—(Sam Rayburn series on rual life ; no. 5)
        Includes bibliographical references (p.   ) and index.
        ISBN 1-58544-250-x (cloth : alk. paper)
                1. Rural churches—Texas—History.   2. Texas—Church history.
        I. Sharpless, Rebecca.   II. Baker, Clark, 1959–   III. Title.   IV. Series.
        BV638.M85   2003
        277.64'08'091734—dc21   2003005001

Information on obtaining exhibition prints of the photographs in this book
may be obtained by contacting the photographer at 2800 Sanger Avenue, Waco, Texas 76707.

CONTENTS

SERIES EDITOR'S FOREWORD

Rock beneath the Sand is the fifth book in the Sam Rayburn Series on Rural Life, a series established on the Texas A&M University-Commerce campus under the auspices of the Texas A&M University Press book publishing program. Designed to be diverse in scope of topics, the series focuses on the eastern half of Texas and the surrounding region. Lois E. Myers and Rebecca Sharpless have provided a remarkable document of open-country churches in one section of this region from the mid-1800s to the present day, based on oral history, field surveys, memoirs, church records, and personal interviews. Accompanied by Clark G. Baker's captivating photographs, this volume records the beginning, apex, and decline of rural churches in McLennan and adjacent counties.

In his collection of lectures, *Myths to Live By,* Joseph Campbell has suggested that one function of religion, myths, and rituals in societies is the universal need for belief in a higher power, a belief which prevents chaos. Myers and Sharpless reflect that need in their account of the effect of rural religion on families and communities through ethnographic methods of research, and they provide an engaging history that reveals the diversity of this selected part of Texas. They include nineteen churches representing five denominations among Southerners, African Americans, Germans, Czechs, Norwegians, and Mexicans. That pioneering spirit and perseverance before, during, and after the Civil War eventually allowed the creation of a sense of unity and bonding, first within their own cultural heritages and later the integration of cultures in small farm communities. The dominant antebellum churches—Methodist, Episcopal, and Southern Baptist—were subsequently joined by other Protestant sects and Roman Catholicism.

The rural churches fostered the family concept, nucleus and extended. Families worked together to build their churches both physically and spiritually, to provide for their pastors, and to help other members of the church family when they were in need. Good country people taught values and a sense of responsibility to their children, and the recorded childhood memories in *Rock beneath the Sand* testify to the positive impact on those citizens who grew up in rural churches. They disclose the positive and enabling effects of their religion and offer a different view from the sometimes negative view of religion in general, and Protestantism in particular, by Southern writers such as Flannery O'Connor.

Further documenting their exploration into the past are a variety of scenes from steeples to signs, chapels to congregations, padres to picnics, cemeteries to celebrations—all richly photographed and thoughtfully presented. The rituals reflected in the pictures link the ties among rural religions in other regions, such as the annual cemetery cleaning tradition, which North Carolina author Clyde Edgerton portrays so well in his fiction, especially in *Raney* and *The Floatplane Notebooks.* The oral history, on which this present volume draws, provides the vibrant sound of voices of individuals who found their identity, who bonded with their community, and who helped harvest a new beginning out of untilled ground. Real names, real people recall real events in this small segment of Texas history.

The changes brought about in the latter half of the twentieth century were not uncommon changes occurring throughout the country. Technology and urbanization created different opportunities for young people who left the agrarian lifestyle. Rural churches' aging congregations were not replenishing themselves. Even when "outsiders" were invited into the churches, the growth was not stimulated by younger members. "Hobby farmers" commuted to their jobs, the primary source of their income. Consolidated school districts with increased activities for students competed for their time, and the church was no longer the center for socialization and unification. Consequently, in this new century, the open-country churches are places on an endangered list.

Myers, Sharpless, and Baker have compiled an informative and interesting history in *Rock beneath the Sand,* one which offers opportunities for similar and extended studies. Teachers, students, and the general reading public will find their work worthwhile. It complements nicely the first four titles in the Sam Rayburn Series on Rural Life and emphasizes again the diversity of topics which its charter envisioned.

—James A. Grimshaw, Jr.

To the casual observer, rural Central Texas offers little except grass and sky. Occasionally, however, the horizon is broken by a structure in the distance: a church, stretching its steeple heavenward. No other structures are in evidence: no schools, no stores, not even a nearby farmhouse. These open-country churches are the remnants of a once-thriving rural culture, which rose and fell with the great Central Texas cotton crops. They persisted despite the dramatic depopulation of rural Texas in the twentieth century. Why are these churches still here? With this simple question, we in the Baylor University Institute for Oral History began searching for answers.

The story of Central Texas agrarian communities and the churches at their centers is, like the region's geography, a study of contrast and conjunction. Geographer Donald W. Meinig described the area as a "varied physical arena of woods and prairies, hills and plains, rich river bottoms and thin-soiled cuestas," which attracted, he added, "more human variety than anywhere else in Texas."[1] A notable example of Central Texas diversity is found in McLennan County, situated where the Brazos River Valley meets the Balcones Fault. East of the Balcones escarpment, the alluvial flood plain provides rich "gumbo" soil, where vegetation thrives. Outside of the river valleys, more than 60 percent of McLennan County lies in the legendary Blackland Prairie, with its distinctive thick clay soil, which is among the most fertile in the United States.[2] Western parts of McLennan County, beyond the uplifting Balcones, occupy the Grand Prairie, with thin soils frequently exposing a hard limestone base. The physical geography of Central Texas ensured that the land would be given over to agriculture as soon as possible.

The development of agriculture on the dissimilar prairies, east and west, gave rise to cultural diversity. Antebellum farmers and planters, along with their slaves, migrated from southeastern states and settled along the river bottoms, laying the foundations for a typically southern society. After the Civil War, new technologies enabled the waxy Blackland to be broken, and the cotton culture, powered by the crop-lien system, dominated the region until the 1930s. As cotton cultivation spread onto the prairies, immigrant farmers of German and Czech descent began arriving. By 1930, they accounted for 6.2 percent of the county's population, a statistically small percentage, yet these farmers from northern and eastern Europe made long-lasting contributions to the region's rural culture, just as they did in Texas counties farther south.[3] Mexicans, arriving as cotton shifted to other parts of Texas, also became an important part of the region's passing rural scene. The story of the Central Texas cotton culture, therefore, is told not only in a southern drawl, but also with German, Czech, and Spanish accents.

Schools, general stores, and gins appeared every few miles amid the cotton fields, and where settlement spread, the Christian gospel followed. Churches, their memberships mirroring the ethnicity of the neighboring families, arose on the open prairies and in small towns. In 1934, Louisa Romans DuPuy identified 190 McLennan County churches in her master's thesis in sociology, and, fortunately, furnished a map with locations of the churches. On DuPuy's map, thirty-two churches originated in open country, outside the environs of the county seat at Waco and apart from the railroad towns and cotton-gin villages scattered across the county.[4] DuPuy's thesis, with its useful map, came to our attention in the Baylor University Institute for Oral History as we conducted research on rural life in our region. Always ready for a field trip, we spent several days in the summer of 1996 touring our county's back roads to discover which of the open-country churches were still holding services after sixty-six years.

Our road trip revealed that of the thirty-two churches that originated in open country, eight remained there, serving without interruption throughout the twentieth century. The continuous open-country churches we found included Baptist churches with Anglo origins at Oak Grove, near China Spring; New Hope, near Riesel; Shiloh, east of Crawford; and Liberty Hill, between Moody and Eddy. We also discovered African American congregations still meeting at Mount Moriah Baptist and Springhill United Methodist, both near Riesel, and former German congregations continuing at Canaan Baptist, west of Crawford, and Meier Settlement United Methodist, near Riesel. At other sites, however, evidence of former churches had disappeared, except perhaps for a cemetery bearing the church name. In some instances, the church houses remained but were vacant and decaying, being slowly erased from the countryside. Two former open-country church

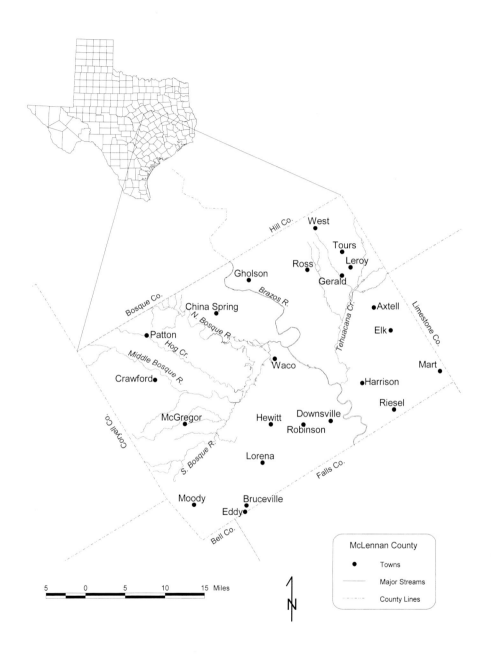

West

Tours
Ross   Leroy
Gholson   Gerald

Hill Co.
Brazos R.
Bosque Co.

China Spring
N. Bosque R.

Patton
Hog Cr.
Middle Bosque R.

Crawford

McGregor

S. Bosque R.

Lorena

Moody   Bruceville
Eddy

Bell Co.

Waco

Hewitt   Downsville
Robinson

Coryell Co.

Axtell
Elk

Tehuacana Cr.

Harrison

Riesel

Mart

Limestone Co.

Falls Co.

5   0   5   10   15   Miles

N

McLennan County

●   Towns

—— Major Streams

– – – County Lines

buildings housed new congregations that had taken over the sites after descendants of the charter members abandoned them.

Along with the open-country churches, we discovered nine additional surviving churches that originated in nineteenth-century villages—cotton-gin communities or rail stations—but by the time we visited them, all signs of their once-thriving neighborhoods stood silent and empty. Among these churches were primarily Anglo congregations at Downsville and Patton, both of which were Baptist. Also surviving beyond their neighborhoods were churches in former African American communities, at Downsville, where Mount Pleasant and Mount Olive Missionary Baptist remained, and at Harrison, still served by Goshen Cumberland Presbyterian Church in America and Pilgrim Rest Baptist. Several churches in former German and Czech communities also survived, including St. Paul's United Church of Christ, at Gerald; St. Martin's Catholic, at Tours; and St. Joseph's Catholic, at Elk.

Interest in open-country churches came naturally for us at Baylor, where our oldest and largest oral history collection concerns the interplay of religion and culture. We also have a longstanding interest in rural life, evidenced by oral histories collected throughout Texas. Interviews gathered by Rebecca Sharpless in Coryell County in 1986 and 1987 from elderly members of Bethlehem Baptist Church, which moved into Gatesville before 1918, gave insight into the church when it was still part of Lincolnville, a rural neighborhood founded in the 1860s by freedpeople. Likewise, Sharpless's 1990 recordings on the life history of Bernice Porter Bostick Weir provided historical background for Liberty Hill Baptist Church, which survived in southeastern McLennan County. Interviews conducted by Lois Myers from 1992 to 1995 with former residents of the South Bosque community, annexed by Waco in 1998, provided information on Harris Creek Baptist Church, representative of rural churches before World War II. Glenn Jonas's 1990 interviews with elderly members of Cego Baptist Church, in Falls County, proved especially timely to our project. Jonas conducted the interviews while serving as the church's pastor and pursuing his doctorate in religion at Baylor. As it turned out, he was the last pastor for Cego Baptist, which closed in 1995. Researchers LaWanda Ball, Jay Butler, Ray Niederer, Suzanne Olsen, and Anne Radford Phillips contributed memoirs that featured members of remaining congregations at Canaan Baptist, Cedar Grove Baptist, Goshen Cumberland Presbyterian Church in America, Majors Chapel

TABLE I. FEATURED OPEN-COUNTRY CHURCHES

Date	Church Name	Type	Community	County
1865	Cedar Grove Baptist	African American	Satin	Falls
1866	Mount Pleasant Missionary Baptist	African American	Downsville	McLennan
1866	Springhill United Methodist	African American	open country	McLennan
1869	Our Savior's Lutheran	Norwegian	Norse	Bosque
1872	Bethlehem Baptist	African American	Lincolnville	Coryell
1872	Harris Creek Baptist	Anglo	South Bosque	McLennan
1874	Goshen CPCA	African American	Harrison	McLennan
1883	Trinity Lutheran	Wendish	open country	Falls
1884	St. Paul's UCC	German	Cego	Falls
1884	Mount Olive Missionary Baptist	African American	Downsville	McLennan
1889	St. John Lutheran	German	Coryell City	Coryell
1893	Canaan Baptist	German	open country	McLennan
1894	St. Paul UCC	German	St. Paul	Falls
1900	St. Paul's UCC	German	Gerald	McLennan
1910	Liberty Hill Baptist	Anglo	open country	McLennan
1911	Cego Baptist	German/Anglo	Cego	Falls
1912	St. Rita's Catholic	Mexican	Satin	Falls
1922	St. Joseph's Catholic	Czech	Elk	McLennan
1924	Birome (Union)	Anglo	Birome	Hill

CPCA=Cumberland Presbyterian Church in America; UCC=United Church of Christ

United Methodist, Mount Olive Missionary Baptist, Mount Pleasant Missionary Baptist, Our Savior's Lutheran, and St. Martin's Catholic.

After our field survey and review of existing memoirs, we embarked on a new oral history project to uncover secrets to the longevity of open-country congregations that still remained. We began contacting pastors and members of churches representing the ethnic and denominational diversity we discovered on our field trip. We learned that in terms of church loyalty, people found county lines invisible and insignificant. Therefore, in order to include a union church that for most of the twentieth century accommodated both Methodists and Baptists, we ventured a few miles north to Birome in Hill County. We also included Lutheran churches located just beyond the McLennan County line in eastern Coryell and northwestern Falls Counties, because only town and city Lutheran churches persisted in our home county. Finally, we stretched our study a few miles south into Falls County on the west side of the Brazos River to a Catholic church founded by Mexican farm laborers. Tape-recorded memoirs gathered from 1996 to 2001 for this specific project by interviewers Jaclyn L. Jeffrey, Marla Pierson Lester, Lois E. Myers, and Rebecca Sharpless highlighted Birome Church, Canaan Baptist, Goshen Cumberland Presbyterian Church in America, Liberty Hill Baptist, St. John Lutheran, St. Joseph's Catholic, St. Paul's United Church of Christ at Cego, St. Paul's United Church of Christ at Gerald, St. Paul United Church of Christ at St. Paul, St. Rita's Catholic, Springhill United Methodist, and Trinity Lutheran.

Oral historians often observe that the best research projects are those which cover subjects for which large bodies of records do not exist, and this project proved to be one of those. The Texas countryside has been underdocumented in general, and its churches have been a part of that underdocumentation. A number of the churches did have privately printed anniversary and dedication booklets written by church history committees. Based on memories of longtime members, church minutes, baptism records, and family histories, these accounts collapsed decades of tradition within a few pages. The books aided our selection of topics and increased our success in adapting topics to individual narrators.

The church pastor was usually our first contact with each church. Locating pastors proved difficult at times, because some rural churches do not have telephone listings. In those cases, driving to the church site and reading the sign in front proved the only way to learn the current pastor's name. In one congregation, an insider told us to begin with selected deacons rather than the pastor. Future interviews within the church family depended, we were told, on their blessing. Once a church agreed to participate in our project, we interviewed the pastor and other key leaders. Our initial interviewees then pointed us to other people in their congregations. We wanted to know why people still attended open-country churches, so we talked almost exclusively to those who stayed. In one instance, we spoke to a member who had left his childhood rural church with some hard feelings, and in another, we interviewed a member who had left for a few years after being disciplined by the church. By the time we spoke with these individuals, their past grievances had been resolved and figured only incidentally in their memories.

Shortly after we began our oral history interviews, we discussed with Clark Baker, Baylor professor of photojournalism, the possibility of his photographing the churches and their congregations. Clark was familiar with oral history research, having been a faculty fellow in the Institute for Oral History, conducting his own interviews about family photography in depression-era Oklahoma.[5] In the following chapters, his photographs depict the open-country churches cherished by the men and women whose oral testimonies comprise the text. His photographer's note describes his thoughts on the relationship between visual evidence and oral testimony.

The photographs portray the ethnic diversity our oral histories revealed among (though not within) open-country congregations in Central Texas. Our narrators opened our eyes to the large roles played by race and ethnicity in the origination and survival of their churches. Rural African Americans formed their own churches almost immediately after emancipation, and all-black congregations continue today, thirty-five years after most Christian denominations began abandoning official policies of racial segregation. Among rural Norwegian, German, and Czech families, children learned English at crossroad schools and parents dealt business in English at the store and gin. At church, however, they sang and prayed and read scriptures in their ancestral tongues until the 1940s. Long past their transitions to English-language services, however, ethnic family groups maintained distinct, separate religious services on Sunday mornings while living in the Anglo mainstream racially, economically, and socially the rest of the week. Newcomers from Mexico continue to arrive to the present day, so separate Spanish-language church services are still common throughout Central Texas.

Having conducted this research, we will no longer view one country church as pretty much just like the next one. Our research illuminated colorful variations in worship styles and church organization among the Christians on the prairies. As in other southern regions, in Central Texas evangelical Protestantism flourished among Anglo and African Americans. Methodists, Baptists, and Cumberland Presbyterians originated antebellum churches and schools in the countryside, followed in the postwar period with the establishment of separate black congregations. Texas Baptists and Methodists created mission societies specifically for German-speaking immigrants, and many of their churches remain intact. The story of the remaining open-country churches in Central Texas, however, is as much about Roman Catholics, Lutherans, and German Evangelical and Reformed congregations as about southern evangelicals. Our research confirmed Meinig's observation of thirty years earlier: "Central Texas is not simply part of the Bible Belt of Southern fundamentalism, nor of the Hispano-Catholic borderlands, nor is it an ethno-religious enclave—it combines important elements of all three."[6] At the crossroads on the Brazos, revivalist appeals to save souls met liturgical reverence for God's glory.

Our interviewees further taught us that many rural churches owe their persistence in large part to women. Women constitute the majority of Sunday morning attendance in rural churches, and they are represented in our oral history interviews by fifty-five voices, compared to thirty-six male interviewees. Gender roles in rural churches changed considerably over time. Within the living memory of some of our narrators, men and women entered through separate doors and sat on opposite sides of the church during worship. Today, women fill pastorates and serve as lay worship leaders and church treasurers.

All our interviewees seemed eager to aid our understanding of their church lives, something that to them had eternal significance. They represented the third to sixth generations of their families in leadership in the same church. Some congregations, we discovered, took their histories almost religiously, especially churches with ethnic roots that had experienced the loss or blending of significant traditions over the last half-century. We appreciate the kindness and generosity shown to us by all our interviewees. Many offered us tours of their churches, walked with us through the cemeteries where their ancestors lay, and showed us family photographs and church records. Almost all our visits in German American homes ended with offers of strong black coffee served with cake or cookies. At least one narrator from each church invited us to join them for Sunday services.

In the twenty-first century, these churches face a fragile existence. Birome Church ceased meeting the year after we interviewed its pastor. Others also will close in the coming years, as devoted but aging members die or move away. Some congregations will forego their traditional character, changing denominational alliance or accepting new leadership from outside the controlling family groups. Each church that remains provides a distinctive bond to a way of life lived by most Texans a century ago. As its steeple lifts our eyes upward from the flat horizon, the persistent open-country church reminds us of our roots deep in the soil beneath our feet.

ACKNOWLEDGMENTS

The heart and soul of this book resides in the voices of the people who talked with us about their lives, families, and churches. Without these people there would be no story, so our appreciation first belongs to them, with sincere hope that we represented their words and feelings accurately and respectfully.

At the Baylor Institute for Oral History we have been gathering firsthand historical accounts from people in various walks of life since 1970. Our oral history interviews are taped, transcribed, and deposited in the Texas Collection archives for scholarly research. On our twenty-fifth anniversary, we invited esteemed oral historian Richard Cándida Smith to evaluate our program and make recommendations for our future. Dr. Smith suggested that in addition to collecting oral histories for other scholars to use, we should make our work more widely known by publishing the results of our interview projects. Within a few weeks of his report, we chose a topic we knew we would enjoy carrying to completion from background research to publication. Thank you, Richard, for your insight and friendship.

When we began investigating the rural church in 1996, we benefited immediately from work completed earlier by researchers on other projects with different aims. In 1934, a woman writing her thesis in sociology composed a map of McLennan County churches and school districts. Little could Louisa Romans DuPuy know how important her map would become for us more than sixty years later. Then, beginning in the 1980s, interviewers talking with Central Texans about rural life included important and useful questions about their churches, some of which are now closed. Toward the end of the project, journalist Marla Pierson Lester extended our research by interviewing additional members of remaining open-country churches. We thank these people for doing research, for asking questions, and for collecting historical matter with timeless significance.

Much of the inspiration for this project initiated with anthropologist Jaclyn L. Jeffrey. Before she moved to Laredo to teach, direct a museum, and complete her dissertation, Jaclyn was our navigator and humorist on our trips across Central Texas in search of surviving rural churches. On a crisp, clear winter night, as we returned from visiting with members of a country church, it was Jaclyn who suggested we stop and look at the stars, and Jaclyn who provided first aid—with a chuckle—when Lois stepped out of the car straight into the bar ditch. We hope Jaclyn enjoys seeing the outcome of this project in which she was such an important starting player.

Baylor University generously encouraged and supported this project all along its journey. The staff and faculty of the Texas Collection granted us access to vertical files and archival materials, and Lisa M. Zygo, of the Center for Applied Geographic and Spatial Research, composed our map of McLennan County. Dr. Wallace Daniel, Dean of the College of Arts and Sciences, granted Clark Baker the release time necessary to complete the photography for this work. The Baylor University Research Committee provided funds for enhancing publication of the photographs. Our colleagues in the Institute for Oral History contributed their special skills. Student staffers and graduate assistants transcribed the tapes and verified the transcripts, under the able supervision of Peggy Kinard and Rebecca Shulda. Editors Kathryn Blakeman, Elinor Mazé, and Ben Vetter each served the roles of advisor, critic, and proofreader over the course of the project. Thank you, Baylor friends, for enabling the execution and completion of this project.

Although documentary photography is a solitary undertaking, according to Clark Baker, good work happens only with the support of good people. He therefore thanks his students, friends, colleagues, and subjects who helped along the way. You know who you are. Clark is forever grateful to his wife, Terri, and their children for their wild, sweet ways. Lois appreciates the hospitality of country churches and, also, the patient support of her husband, Dennis Myers, who listened with genuine interest to rural church stories for six years. Becca thanks Tom Charlton and remembers her Sharpless grandparents, who are buried in open-country church cemeteries four hundred miles apart.

Working together on this project has been a pleasure for all three of us.

ROCK BENEATH THE SAND

CHAPTER 1

Rural Life and Religion in Central Texas

*I*MAGINE A LANDSCAPE RIPPLING WITH GRASS, watered by small streams, broken in places by limestone ledges. From northwest to southeast flows a river, wide and powerful after heavy rains, shallow and sluggish during dry spells. At widely spaced intervals along the river's path are natural fords, an exposed rock outcropping or an abrupt fall in the river, facilitating crossings for nomadic animals and peoples. Imagine a land with searing hot summers and mild winters, punctuated by blue northers, potent cold fronts sweeping down from wide plains to the north. Imagine this, and you will conjure the landscape now known as Central Texas as it appeared to the native people who populated the area for more than ten thousand years before the earliest Anglo American settlers entered the region in the early nineteenth century.

At the opening of the twenty-first century, the blue bowl of the sky still covers the prairie and shines brilliantly in the river's waters, but all is not as it once was. From the hard-rock crossing on the ancient river, now tamed by mechanized dams, a city sprawls in all directions. The broad swath of an interstate highway intersects the river just a few hundred feet from the old crossing, rushing millions of people and the goods they consume on their ways from Mexico to Canada. Bands of concrete highways and steel railroads, lined by buzzing communication wires, connect the city with small towns across the prairies. Between highways, fences crisscross the countryside, separating cattle from fields of corn and hay.

Here and there across the remaining open country a solitary steeple casts its shadow on the prairie. Out on a highway stretching between towns, an old iron bell hangs from a post in the yard of a small white church, easily overlooked by passing drivers. Viewed on the wide horizon, the physical presence of singular churches in the open country appears insignificant, but they are powerful representatives of a century and a half of human history on the prairie. In between the two eras of grass—the native bluestem and the cultivated hay—lies the story of the rise and fall of an agricultural people. Their story is a common one across the southern United States, where, in the latter decades of the nineteenth century, innumerable hamlets sprang up and briefly flourished.[1] Families scattered over the neighboring prairies, and the local school, church, and general store became their central points of contact with one another.

These villages have always been in a state of change, however. As early as the late nineteenth century, railroads bypassed many of them, and, later, automobiles and better roads improved access to the amenities of town. The people gave their all to cotton, and cotton abandoned them and moved west, where the flat terrain better accommodated broad-scale mechanized agriculture. Country schools consolidated with town schools, machinery replaced people on the farms, and labor-needy industry enticed young people to the city. Crossroads stores, where tenants and share-croppers once pledged their crops in exchange for seed and supplies, closed as the people left. As the city and towns widened, they swallowed the nearest prairie communities and turned the next-nearest into suburbs. In some of the remaining hamlets, even the churches disappeared. Time, aided by storms and fires, has demolished the physical remains of abandoned schools, stores, and churches, leaving the sites of many former crossroads communities indistinguishable from the pastures around them. A state historical marker or road sign remains as the lone testimony for other one-time hamlets. For many, only a cemetery endures.

How, then, does the twenty-first century account for the presence of those occasional surviving steeples on the prairie? Why did a significant number of congregations founded in nineteenth-century communities persist in open country after all else disappeared save for people's memories? To answer these questions, one must return to the origins of the churches. The faith that inspired the first generation to create and perpetuate Christian congregations along the river bottoms and on the prairies of north Central Texas became the foundation for their staying power.

ST. PAUL UNITED CHURCH OF CHRIST, NEAR MARLIN

Water, grass, and game lured ancient people across the natural fords on the wide river that the Spanish, who laid claim to the area in the early sixteenth century, named Los Brazos de Dios, the arms of God. The Spanish left north Central Texas, however, to the American Indians, who by the early nineteenth century were mostly members of the Tonkawa, Waco, or Tawakoni tribes. From

the west, the Comanche made their presence felt by sending occasional raiding parties into the region. Before 1845, and the achievement of statehood for Texas, Anglo settlers crept hesitantly up the Brazos, stopping near Fort Milam at the falls on the Brazos. With statehood, federal soldiers stationed at Fort Gates guarded the western fringes of settlement, and pioneers began entering the river bottoms above the falls, occupying first those lands closest to rivers and creeks. About a dozen Anglo families established homes above a hard-rock crossing thirty miles north of the falls, near a spring-fed campsite formerly occupied by the Waco tribe, whose name the newcomers adopted for their community. Families moved into the bottomlands above Waco Village, establishing homesteads on the branches of the Bosque River and on Hog Creek. These earliest settlers were subsistence farmers who domesticated wild cattle and horses for their use and hunted game to supplement their diet and provide pelts for trade.[2]

Within one week in January 1850, the Texas legislature created Falls County, Bell County, and McLennan County, which included the area that in 1854 became Bosque County. Creations of Hill and Coryell Counties followed in 1853 and 1854. A rapid influx of settlement into Central Texas ensued. By 1860, McLennan County had grown to a population of 6,206, establishing itself as the most populous district between Travis and Dallas Counties.[3] The majority of settlers came from older communities in Texas or from the southeastern United States, particularly the Carolinas, Tennessee, Georgia, Alabama, and Mississippi. Beginning in 1854, Norwegian migration into Bosque County provided the first exception to Anglo American settlement. The Norwegians had arrived in Henderson County in 1845, and, while they found the East Texas soil to be profitable, heat and disease took its toll among them. Leader Cleng Peerson discovered a better climate on the high prairies west of the Bosque River, and in 1854 eight families and two single men followed him there to homestead public lands available in the newly organized county.[4]

Among the newcomers from southeastern states were slaves, brought as laborers to break the sod, cultivate the crops, and build their owners' houses. Plantation culture arrived late in Central Texas, but at the outbreak of the Civil War, its progress was notably successful. Anglo yeoman farmers greatly outnumbered the slaveholders, just as they did elsewhere in the South; in Central Texas, 82 percent of all farmers did not own slaves.[5] Even so, between 1850 and 1860, the number of slaves in McLennan County increased from forty-nine to 2,105, and bona fide plantations appeared on the Brazos flood plain.[6] From established plantations in the Deep South, planters carried wagonloads of slaves and farm implements onto the river bottoms below Waco. By 1860, slaves accounted for more than 38 percent of the McLennan County population and more than 43 percent of the population of Falls County.[7] While more than half of McLennan County slave owners held four slaves or fewer, 9 percent could be classified as planters, holding more than twenty slaves. Four planters held between sixty and seventy-two slaves.[8] Clearly, the peculiar institution was flourishing in Central Texas.

Heavily invested in slavery, white Central Texans supported secession with little resistance, giving their young men and their provisions in the war effort.[9] As the westernmost point of the

Confederacy, Texas provided shelter for slaveholders trying to hold onto their human property in the face of northern invasion. During the Civil War, the slave population of Central Texas expanded by 122 percent, as planters and farmers brought slaves to Texas by the thousands while Union forces advanced into the Confederacy. Between 1860 and 1864, the number of slaves in McLennan, Falls, Bosque, and Coryell Counties jumped from 4,207 to 9,356. After the Civil War, many of these so-called refugeed slaves remained in Texas, providing the setting for the development of strong black communities after the war.[10]

In antebellum Central Texas, the rural population outnumbered residents in the county seats two to one. Farmers and planters set about to replicate the agrarian culture of their southern heritage, including an evangelical religious tradition. As southerners migrated from the eastern seaboard, they left behind the quiet formality of the Anglican Church. Moving across the lower and middle South to Texas, they found solace in the midst of frontier hardships in the promise of a better life in heaven preached fervently by the occasional Baptist or Methodist minister. The Second Great Awakening, sometimes called the Great Revival, ensured that the major impulse of new communities would be evangelical in nature. Methodism proved to be highly effective, as their circuit-riding ministers spread out among sparse settlements. Baptists also flourished, in part due to their emphasis on individual expression, exhibited in the principle of the priesthood of the believer and a decentralized church structure. Religion in the rural South emphasized the importance of each individual's having a direct experience of God's grace and choosing independently to follow God. The emphasis on individual experience also led to the evangelical church's focus on moral accountability, with behaviors such as drinking, dancing, and swearing considered grievous sins.[11]

With a few exceptions, then, the story of antebellum churches in rural Central Texas belongs to the Methodist Episcopal Church, South, and the Southern Baptist Convention, which separated from their northern, antislavery counterparts in 1844 and 1845, respectively. Adherents of the two denominations disagreed with one another on doctrinal matters, but they held in common a full endorsement of the plantation economy, slavery, and states rights. On the eve of the Civil War, Methodists and Baptists claimed within their folds about 9 percent of the population of McLennan County. While this figure seems low by contemporary standards, it was typical of life in antebellum Texas.[12]

PILGRIM REST BAPTIST CHURCH, HARRISON

Methodists made early and successful inroads into Texas. They traced their beginnings to 1815, when Methodist circuit rider William Stevenson crossed the Red River into Spanish Texas. By 1840, there were sufficient numbers of Methodists in the new Republic of Texas to form the Texas Conference, with 1,648 white and 230 black members, served by seventeen preachers traveling fourteen circuits. Each Methodist circuit rider covered a wide territory, preaching at a different settlement every week, holding revival meetings and performing weddings and funerals as needed. In 1860, 39,021 Texans claimed membership in the Methodist Episcopal Church, South. Of that number, 8,360 were black. From the 1840s Methodists appointed full-time white missionaries to the growing African American population in Texas. Until 1859 some Methodist congregations allowed their black members to meet separately, under the preaching of a slave licensed by the conference. As fears grew of slave rebellions aided by northern abolitionists, including clergy of the Methodist Episcopal Church, the 1859 session of the Texas Conference recommended an end to separate meetings and discontinuance of licensing or renewing licenses for black preachers.[13]

Baptists were likewise among the earliest Anglo settlers in Spanish Texas, and they opened the first known Sunday schools in the colony, beginning in 1829 in San Felipe. Organized in the early 1830s, the first two Baptist churches in Texas followed the independent Hardshell or Predestinarian Baptist tradition, which opposed any hint of corporate effort, including Sunday schools, denominations, and missions. Within the next decade, however, Baptists with missionary zeal, well organized to support evangelistic efforts in new territories, began to outnumber their antimissionary brethren. Foremost among the early Baptist missionaries was Z. N. Morrell, who arrived in 1836 and spent the next fifty years spreading the gospel throughout Texas.[14] In 1840, three Baptist churches created Union Association, their first regional organization, and appointed missionaries to frontier settlements. The next year, the newly established Texas Baptist Education Society began formulating a charter for the first major university of the Republic of Texas. In early 1845, months before the annexation of Texas by the United States, Baylor University opened in Independence, Texas. Later in 1845, the Home Mission Board of the recently organized Southern Baptist Convention sent its first two missionaries to the state. By 1848, six regional associations aligned to form the Baptist State Convention, and by 1849, Baptists claimed to have twenty-nine preachers covering the settled parts of the state. Between 1845 and 1860, Texas Baptists opened five hundred churches affiliated with twenty-four regional associations.[15]

At its organizational meeting in 1848 the Baptist State Convention addressed the need for white missionaries to "use every exertion and embrace every opportunity to preach to the colored people," and encouraged pastors "to appropriate a part of each Sabbath to their spiritual welfare." The same speaker, however, predicated his enthusiasm for converting slaves with the caveat, "we religiously believe that slavery is amply and fully sustained by the Bible."[16] Baptist pastors baptized slaves and allowed them to sit in designated places in their churches, and planters paid white preachers a little extra for evangelizing their slaves. A few Baptist planters read the Bible to their slaves, but they generally refused to teach them to read, encouraging dependence on white interpretations of Scripture, especially in regard to race equality and slave-master relationships. A few separate slave churches organized on large plantations under white missionary leadership. As pre-war anxiety increased, however, Baptists, like their Methodist cohorts, tightened control over slave religion, halting the black Christians' movement toward autonomy.[17]

In antebellum Central Texas, scattered Anglo families formed ties with one another, gathering when possible to socialize and catch up on news. In most communities, a first collective act was building a one-room log schoolhouse, which also served the neighborhood as an election site and, on one or two Sundays each month, a place for Christians to gather to listen to itinerant preachers. In the absence of a schoolhouse and circuit rider, a family might open

GRAVE MARKER, ST. MARTIN'S CATHOLIC CEMETERY, TOURS

its home on Sundays for the neighbors to gather for Bible reading and prayer. Annual camp meetings concentrated preaching, singing, praying, and winning converts within a space of seven to ten days. Preachers chose sites out in the country where water and shade were abundant, and families came in wagons and pitched tents. One observer admitted that the country revivals were as much about "socializing" as about "spiritualizing," but added that they helped blend rural neighbors into informal congregations that eventually became organized churches.[18]

Methodism grew rapidly among the Anglos in town, so that by 1858, the Waco church reported 158 members and forty-two probationary members, served by three local preachers. Out in the countryside, however, the Waco circuit spread to all settlements from Gatesville to Waco to Marlin and reported only fifteen white members, twenty-seven black members, and two black probationary members.[19] Lack of membership did not indicate lack of enthusiasm, however. When settlers heard of a Methodist preacher's presence in their vicinity, they traveled great distances over the prairie to hear him. James H. Addison, Waco district preacher in 1854, wrote to his brother one Monday that on the previous day he "had the pleasure of holding forth to quite a fine audience of Brazos, Bosque and surrounding country, in a little bit of a stick and dirt school house about ten miles above the capitol of McLennan Co. to wit Waco." In the same letter, Addison mentioned that the coming Thursday he would return to the country to perform a marriage and that he had attended a "very fine camp meeting" out in the country, where several families brought tents and stayed for the week-long event. During the camp meeting, forty-two converts joined the Methodist church, inspiring Addison to claim, "Methodism received a fresh impetus, and I think it is well established that nothing can move it now. The combined powers of the Baptists and the Devil will be unavailing towards shaking the fabric thus reared."[20]

Despite Addison's optimism, Baptists gradually outgrew Methodists in rural Central Texas. Baptist farmers were among the first settlers in McLennan County. In 1849, Israel Washington Speegle, originally from North Carolina, migrated from Missouri and established a farm on the South Bosque River. He opened a blacksmith shop to serve the neighboring farms and built a home for his wife and eight children. Soon he invited his neighbors over to meet for Baptist worship services.[21] In Waco, three years later, four Southern Baptists organized the First Baptist Church, using the Methodist building for its meetings and the Brazos River for its baptistery.[22] By 1859,

Baptists reported rural congregations at Bold Springs, Union Springs, and White Rock in north-eastern McLennan County, and, just across the Leon River in Coryell County, at Onion Springs.[23]

Meeting in a schoolhouse in northwestern Falls County in the 1850s, the Cow Bayou Baptist Church kept minutes and baptism records that provide some insight into the functions of these early churches in setting moral standards among their communities. Typical of other Baptist churches of its day, Cow Bayou practiced discipline among members reported for "unbecoming behavior," such as dancing, drinking or selling alcohol, swearing, and stealing cattle. When disciplined members repented before the gathered congregation and asked forgiveness, the church restored their full fellowship. The church often served as a jury, settling disputes between members.[24]

In 1860, nine Central Texas churches created the Waco Baptist Association and assumed patronage of Waco University and Classical School, established as a male preparatory school in 1857. Waco University became coeducational in 1866 and operated until 1886, when it merged with Baylor University upon its relocation from Independence to Waco.[25] The longstanding presence in Waco of Baptist higher education furnished generations of pastors for regional churches, provided local Baptists access to the denomination's top Texas leaders, and helped solidify Baptist dominance in Central Texas.

Apart from the few statistics reported by Methodists, specific information on the religious lives of Central Texas slaves is lost. Only rarely did Texas Baptist churches keep count of their slave memberships. The Waco Baptist Association not only failed to keep records of baptized slaves but also failed to persuade a white missionary to preach among them.[26] The lack of Baptist efforts among slaves in McLennan County might be explained by the fact that of eight resident Baptist pastors in the county, five were slaveholders.[27] In 1864, the association report on missions among the slaves stated succinctly, "Some of them attend our white services, some have regular special services, some have no services. We have no missionary among them, but we ought to have."[28]

In some rural locations, Methodists and Baptists shared a meeting space and attended services when an itinerant preacher of either denomination arrived on Sundays. At Bosque (later Bosqueville), located between bends in the Brazos and Bosque rivers about four miles northwest of Waco, Methodists, who constituted a church in 1853, and Baptists, who formed a congregation in 1854, shared a log school building. These two churches were the first organized and appear to be the

GRAVE MARKER, ST. MARTIN'S CATHOLIC CEMETERY, TOURS

longest-lasting rural congregations in McLennan County. Later, these Methodists and Baptists shared the building of the Bosqueville College and Seminary, a nonsectarian school operated by a Cumberland Presbyterian minister from 1858 to 1865. Ten years later, the Bosqueville Methodist Church erected a building apart from the Baptists.[29] In 1855, another antebellum Methodist-Baptist union church met in a schoolhouse in the southwestern quadrant of McLennan County in the growing community of Perry.[30]

During the Civil War, Baptist and Methodist expansion in Texas came to a standstill. State organizations suspended printing of denominational newspapers and church-sponsored schools lost their males students to military service. Able-bodied preachers followed the Confederate army to serve as soldiers, chaplains, or missionaries. The preachers left behind were older men who spent their fading energies providing for the basic needs of their families and holding services within walking distance of their homes. They complained to their denominational leaders about moral decline and lack of discipline within their communities. Missionary efforts concentrated on the spiritual and physical needs of the soldiers. The best horses and mules went to the cause of war, and without their most useful means of transportation, circuit riders curtailed their work among isolated settlers in the countryside. Also, the loss of military presence in the westernmost settlements of the state left travelers in those districts vulnerable to Comanche assault, thereby inhibiting itenerant evangelism. The Federal blockade along the Texas coastline prevented missionaries from obtaining new Bibles and churches from importing manufactured construction materials. Christians collected used Bibles for distribution to the soldiers and watched their church buildings and furnishings fall into disrepair.[31]

For farm families waiting out the war at home, community gatherings for prayer and Bible study increased in importance. Letters exchanged between Patience Crain Black and her husband James, a Confederate volunteer serving on the Gulf Coast, provide a glimpse into Christian life among rural Central Texans during the Civil War. While her husband was away, Patience Black lived with her parents, Joel and Sarah Crain, who settled in 1855 along the confluence of Harris Creek and the South Bosque River west of Waco. Women, children, and the few older men left behind met on Sundays in neighboring homes to exchange news, read the Bible, and pray and sing together. Private devotional lives deepened. Patience Black attended neighborhood preaching services, often led by laypersons, and found solace in reading her Bible at home.[32]

After the end of the Civil War, north Central Texas burst from the gradual settlement of earlier decades into an era of expansion that brought dramatic changes to the economic, social, and religious landscape. Reconstruction was generally ineffective, and white planters and merchants resumed their hegemony with little trouble.[33] For freedpeople, the euphoria of emancipation quickly gave way to the necessity of finding a way to earn a living. Most had no assets to buy land and accepted work for wages or shares, often from their former masters. Many left the area, soon replaced by other African Americans, migrating from the Southeast in search of a better life. They found themselves strictly segregated, the boundaries of race enforced by violence.[34] Former river bottom plantations broke down into small farms rented to tenants and sharecroppers of both races.

Homestead laws opened public lands for settlement and provided fresh starts for thousands of newcomers streaming out of devastated states to the east. In January 1870, the Waco Suspension Bridge became the first bridge to cross the nine-hundred-mile length of the Brazos River, funneling over its span multitudes of westward-moving Americans plus hundreds of European immigrants. The number of inhabitants of McLennan, Bosque, and Coryell Counties doubled between 1860 and 1870, and doubled again by 1880. With an 1880 population of 26,934, McLennan County was one of the most populous counties in Texas. Falls County experienced tremendous growth, also, with its population almost tripling between 1860 and 1870, and growing to 16,240 by 1880.[35]

The main attraction for migrants to north Central Texas in the mid-1870s was the spread of commercial agriculture beyond river bottom plantations onto the wide prairies. The arrival of iron and steel plows made it possible to break the tough native sod, and barbed wire allowed the separation of livestock and crops. Cotton, the money crop for the lower American South, thrived in Central Texas, where the climate supported an eight-month growing season. Just-sufficient rainfall in most years supplemented the natural fertility of the soils. The prairie became a patchwork of cotton farms. One-room schools arose along rough wagon trails to provide basic education to farm children. Every few miles a store opened, where local farmers traded milk, eggs, chickens, vegetables, and fruits, for staple groceries and supplies. Cotton gins appeared in antebellum hamlets or at crossroads where new communities developed. Among these other signs of settlement, Christian farm families organized congregations and erected churches. Most continued to share preachers with other churches, but a few attained full-time pastors. Diversity entered the rural landscape, and newcomers introduced a variety of religious denominations to Central Texas.

Bosqueville prospered with the cotton boom and continued to support Anglo Baptist and Methodist churches, with an African American Baptist church soon appearing there. Methodists

HORNE CEMETERY, NEAR MOODY

opened a church in Speegleville, where the Baptists who once met in the Speegle home also organized as a church and built a meetinghouse. Along the Brazos and Bosque rivers, new gin centers developed at China Spring, Erath, Rock Creek, Gholson, and Robinsonville, accompanied in each instance by a Southern Baptist church. Methodists also established churches at China Spring and Gholson; Presbyterians and German Evangelicals at Robinsonville; and Disciples of Christ at China Spring. South of Robinsonville, the gin community at Rosenthal supported a Church of Christ, a Methodist church, and an African American Baptist church. German and Czech Catholics established churches at Tours and Elk, their cotton centers. Willow Grove, an African American community, prospered around its gin, school, and Baptist church.[36]

The railroad played a crucial part in the development of Central Texas communities. Between 1872 and 1888, five railroads entered the area and competed to carry away farm products, greatly reducing costs, expanding markets to a national level, and contributing to the ascendancy of cotton. Settlements nearest the railroad stops attracted new businesses almost entirely related to agriculture, including stockyards, gristmills, cotton gins, and cottonseed oil presses. In other locations, new town sites developed at stations along the rail lines. Communities bypassed by the railroads disappeared. Many whole settlements packed up and moved into the nearest rail town.[37]

In McLennan County alone, twenty-two towns and villages arose at rail stations outside Waco. By 1930, nineteen Southern Baptist and thirteen Methodist Episcopal, South, churches existed in the rail towns. In some cases, their core memberships derived from older congregations that moved into town when the railroad arrived.[38] In two rail stop villages, South Bosque and Leroy, the two major southern denominations had union churches. By 1930, six rail towns had Churches of Christ, five had Disciples of Christ churches, and four had Presbyterian congregations. African Americans added another fourteen Baptist, eight Methodist, and three Cumberland Presbyterian churches to the rail towns and villages. The town of Mart supported the widest variety of churches outside of Waco, including an Episcopal church, one black Church of God in Christ, an unidentified African American mission church, and a Mexican Presbyterian church. German language churches in rail towns included Evangelical and Methodist churches at Riesel and Lutheran congregations in McGregor and Battle. The Roman Catholic church in West served a large Czech parish.[39]

Beyond cotton-gin and rail communities, on open prairie in the heart of cotton country, thirty-two other churches appeared by 1930. The churches reflected the ethnicity of the founding families—Anglo, African American, or European—and ethnicity, in turn, influenced denominational affiliation. Twenty of the open-country churches served Anglo families: twelve Baptist churches, seven Methodist, one Presbyterian, and one Church of Christ. Rural African American families found fellowship in three Baptist churches and three Methodist churches in open country. German farmers worshipped in their native language at one Baptist, one Methodist, one Lutheran, and two Evangelical churches in open country.[40]

Rural Christians organized congregations and erected humble worship sites with the conviction that a strong, caring divinity would carry them through each crisis and reward them with a better life in the world to come. Their church provided a gathering place to read scriptures and sing hymns in the language of their ancestors, to teach their children the principles of their faith, to pray for relief when there was too little or too much rain, and to express thanksgiving when their prayers were answered. The following accounts describe the beginnings of representative churches founded in open country during cotton's primacy.

After the Civil War, rural Central Texas continued to be primarily Anglo and primarily Southern Baptist. Typical of other majority churches of the period, the Harris Creek Church saw good times come, go, and come again. In the 1850s, farmers had settled along the narrow floodplain of the South Bosque River, just below the slopes of the escarpment west of Waco. As Patience Crain Black revealed in her Civil War letters, some South Bosque families had gathered for worship services in homes. In 1872, Aquilla and Delila Jones deeded land for a church and school alongside a South Bosque River tributary named Harris Creek. The deed specified that the Methodist, Baptist, Presbyterian, and Christian denominations share the property, "each having their Sabbath in each month."[41] The Cotton Belt Railroad established a stop at South Bosque in 1882, and by 1900, the community boasted four general stores, a post office, rail station, public school, blacksmith shop, brickyard, two cotton gins, a gristmill, three medical doctors, seven saloons, a community band, and a basketball team.[42]

When eleven-year-old Geneva Maxwell Russell moved to South Bosque in 1918, Baptists held services in a two-room building that had served until the previous year as the local schoolhouse. The church met twice monthly, usually under the preaching of a Baylor University ministerial student who rode the train from Waco to South Bosque for the day, led morning services, lunched in a member's home, and preached again in the evening before returning to Waco. In 1921, at age fourteen, Russell became a Sunday-school teacher for younger children. Sunday school met every week and consisted of four classes—adult, young people, junior, and children—gathered by age into the four corners of a single large room. The other room in the former school building housed the worship service held every other week. Worshippers sat on wooden slat benches, kept warm with a single coal-burning, potbellied stove, and sang to the strains of a pump organ.

By 1928, the Harris Creek congregation saw the need for better facilities and embarked on a fund-raising campaign. Geneva Russell, by then a twenty-one-year-old schoolteacher, spent the

PRAIRIE CHAPEL SCHOOL, NEAR CRAWFORD

summer walking door-to-door through the neighborhood asking for donations for a new church building. Completed within a year, the new structure provided a place for funerals and weddings for the entire community. Harris Creek remained mostly Baptist until 1932, when the Methodists began sending preachers to the community on alternating Sundays, thereby allowing the community its first opportunity to have church every week. Methodist and Baptist young people both attended Sunday school in the mornings and Baptist Young People's Union in the evenings. The denominations were so compatible that the only difference Geneva Russell noticed between the Methodist and Baptist services came at communion time. The Methodist preacher opened the Lord's Supper to all in attendance, but the Baptist preacher limited the observance to Baptist members only.[43]

For African Americans, promises of economic and political advancement failed to materialize after the Civil War, but former slaves assumed control over their families and gradually formed communities. Although their percentage among the region's population declined with the passing of each decade after emancipation, African Americans made significant and long-lasting contributions to the religious landscape of rural Central Texas.[44] One of the first expressions of freedom for emancipated Christians was to assemble publicly for worship and to organize churches under their own control. In the realm of religion, they achieved a degree of self-determination denied them in all other aspects of life. Christian freedpeople first met for worship in clearings or under brush arbors, open-sided tabernacles roofed with tree branches or any other material at hand. As the congregations grew, they constructed one-room log buildings. Eventually, they obtained title to property and built wooden frame churches. In most cases, the schools and churches shared the same building. The church became the social center for all African Americans within walking distance. Here they held revivals and organized mutual aid societies and fraternal lodges. The entire neighborhood showed up at church to celebrate the anniversary of the announcement of emancipation in Texas with annual Juneteenth picnics. Neighbors soon became kin as young people married within the congregational circle.[45]

Across the postbellum South, more African Americans embraced Baptist theology and polity than any other Christian denomination. The historic Baptist emphasis on congregational self-rule allowed each black church to call its preacher, develop its leadership, and voluntarily align, if desired, with other black churches into associations and state conventions.[46] By 1890, 54 percent of southern African Americans who held membership in all-black churches were Baptists, and in Texas, the figure was 60 percent.[47]

The earliest African American Baptist congregations in McLennan County developed along the Brazos River bottoms south of Waco, among tenants and sharecroppers, many of whom eventually owned land. Initially, these churches received assistance from white Christians, even some who were former slaveholders, but the black Baptists survived and prospered independently, completely autonomous and totally segregated. In 1874, the deacons of Pilgrim Rest Baptist Church received three acres of land located near Shaw's Creek on the east side of the Brazos from James Edward Harrison, a former planter and Confederate general. Harrison left public record that he gave the land for use as a church, cemetery, and school "for and in consideration of the respect I have for the religion of Jesus Christ, the desire I have to advance his cause in this world, and the love I have in my heart for God."[48] On the west side of the Brazos, in 1866, families organized Mount Pleasant Missionary Baptist Church with assistance from an Anglo minister.[49] Twenty years later, trustees of the church bought five acres of land surrounding their meeting place from former slaveholder J. W. Downs. The church paid $123 for the property, giving eighty dollars in cash and signing a promissory note for the remainder.[50] In 1884, members of Mount Pleasant founded a second church in a brush arbor three miles to the southeast. In 1889, on land donated by former slave owners Davis R. and Loulie Earle Gurley, the new congregation erected a log building and took the name Mount Olive Baptist Church. By the end of World War I, a frame building with a bell tower replaced the older structure.[51]

Beyond the river bottoms, on the prairies, other African American Baptists moved into the area to farm cotton. Buck Manning and A. W. Crawford and their families migrated from Mississippi to Bosque County in the vicinity of Valley Mills. They organized a Baptist church, and Crawford served as the preacher. In 1874, Manning homesteaded 320 acres draining into Hog Creek in western McLennan County. Over the next twenty years, he and his wife Lucy deeded portions of their land to their descendants and to other black families. The Mannings also donated land near a creek for a Baptist church, and the new congregation chose Willow Grove for its name. In 1921, trustees of Willow Grove Baptist Church purchased one acre of the old Buck Manning homestead on higher ground for a new church site.[52]

ST. RITA'S CATHOLIC
CHURCH, SATIN

The Methodist church also proved attractive to African Americans. By 1870, the Methodist Episcopal Church, South, encouraged its black members to join the newly organized Colored (later Christian) Methodist Episcopal Church in America (CME). No evidence exists to suggest any CME presence in the Central Texas countryside, however.[53] More successful in Central Texas were the missionary efforts of the northern Methodist Episcopal Church and the African Methodist Episcopal Church (A.M.E.), created in 1816 in Philadelphia by and for African Americans.

Until 1939, Central Texas black Methodist Episcopal churches fell under the direction of the West Texas Conference, which in 1875 reported having 6,729 members served by sixty-six preachers.[54] Among those early Methodists were members of a congregation organized in 1866 by black sharecroppers and day laborers in a small log house on a hill overlooking a running spring on the eastern side of the Brazos River bottom. In 1878, five trustees and stewards of the church bought three acres of land for twenty dollars, and over the next two years Springhill Methodist Church determined its name and built its first frame building. The church, its adjoining cemetery, and a schoolhouse served as the community center for neighboring African American families. The church also provided refuge for African American families displaced from their homes by overflows of the Brazos River and its tributaries. For many nights, until the waters receded, families from riverside neighborhoods slept on the church's wooden benches. Throughout the cotton boom, more black families moved onto area farms, enriching Springhill church with faithful members. In 1936, nearby Rising Sun Methodist Church, having lost much of its membership to the city, consolidated with Springhill.[55]

The African Methodist Episcopal Church also made successful inroads among Central Texans, strengthened after 1877 by the presence in Waco of A.M.E.'s Paul Quinn College. Pastors in training at the school supplied the pulpits of small churches, and lay leaders from area churches benefited from educational opportunities through the college. In 1887, Holder's Chapel A.M.E. Church in the community of Harrison received an acre of land from African American landowners Immanuel and Julia Snowden. The founding family, the Holders, came to the area from Tennessee, brought as tenant farmers by former plantation master James Edward Harrison to replace other freed laborers who had left the Brazos River bottoms upon their emancipation.[56]

The presence in Central Texas of several African American churches belonging to the

Cumberland Presbyterian Church in America (CPCA) began among Anglo slaveholders who migrated into Bosque and Coryell Counties. Indigenous to the South, a product of the frontier revivals of 1800, the Cumberland Presbyterian Church prospered in antebellum Tennessee, Kentucky, and northern Alabama.[57] In the 1850s, Chester Calhoun Sadler, from Tennessee, founded a Cumberland Presbyterian church at the settlement of Rainey's Creek, just west of the Coryell-McLennan County line. The congregation had twenty white members, mostly members of the Sadler family, and five slave members, including Susan Thompson and her three children, brought to Rainey's Creek in 1853 by their master, John Kincaid Sadler.[58] Following emancipation, Susan Thompson married James B. Sadler, a self-educated teacher and preacher, who family tradition claims came to Bosque County from Tennessee after the Civil War with his former owner, a physician also named James Sadler. James B. and Susan T. Sadler made contact with other African American members of the Cumberland Presbyterian Church living in Central Texas. In 1876, three black ministers, separating their congregations from the Waco Presbytery, created the Brazos River Presbytery of the Colored Cumberland Presbyterian Church, which held its first meeting in Bosqueville the following year.[59] From these roots grew CPCA churches at Harrison, Elm Mott, and Waco in McLennan County, and Rock Springs, Clifton, and Meridian in Bosque County.[60] In 1897, the Harrison church, later named Goshen CPCA, received thirty acres of land willed to the congregation upon the death of African American landowner Immanuel Snowden, and in 1938, Goshen transferred the property to the Brazos River Presbytery.[61]

Much of the fuel for the late-nineteenth-century Central Texas growth in population and economy stemmed from the influx of European immigrants. Immigration scholar, Jay P. Dolan, discovered that "religion was central to the immigrant experience," and churches appeared along with homes and schools in their communities. Economic, political, and social advancement in their new homeland required immigrants to assimilate into the dominant culture. In religious matters, however, they managed to maintain separateness and distinctiveness in an atmosphere that fostered continuity of their native language and customs. "If there was no church," Dolan stated, "there was no colony; and without a colony, the culture of the immigrants would have disappeared."[62] The persistence of multiple congregations founded by immigrants in rural Central Texas confirms the centrality of religion in their lives.

ELK STORE, ELK

By 1870, after sixteen years of settlement in Bosque County, Norwegians numbered 716, or 14 percent of the county's population. The vast majority of these Norwegian Texans were Lutherans. Until 1869, Lutheran ministers visited Bosque County only occasionally, so laymen performed baptisms. Families gathered in homes when possible to read the Bible and the Lutheran catechism. In 1867, they elected officers and deacons and began seeking a resident pastor, a process that took two years. The first organized Norwegian Lutheran congregation in Texas, the church met in the local schoolhouse until it completed its own building in 1876. In 1886, the congregation took the name Our Savior's Lutheran Church. The community surrounding the church became known as Norse. As successive generations spread east and west, the Norwegians formed new Lutheran congregations, including St. Olaf's, organized in 1886 west of Norse, and Trinity, eastward in Clifton, in 1907. Our Savior's Lutheran resisted affiliation with a synod until 1901, when the church joined the Norwegian Lutheran Synod.[63]

As the Norwegians reached their second generation in Bosque County, other European immigrants arrived in Central Texas. From the 1870s, German farmers settled in the four corners of McLennan County. First came farmers migrating from counties in the German Belt of south Central Texas, principally from Washington, Fayette, and Austin Counties. Once settled, these farmers sent to Germany for relatives and friends to join them. Dozens of young men came as farmhands and tenants and worked their way up to land ownership. By 1930 the McLennan County population born in Germany numbered 758 and the population with one or both parents born in Germany numbered 3,003, or 3 percent of the total county population. Czechs arrived on the heels of the Germans and became the second largest immigrant group in McLennan County. In 1930, the county census recorded 560 persons born in Czechoslovakia (Bohemia or Moravia), and 1,776 persons with Czech parentage, representing 1.8 percent of the total county population.[64]

During Reconstruction, the Texas state legislature opened for sale 220,000 acres of former public domain lands in McLennan County, and homesteaders with German origins arrived to claim their portions. They came with Catholic or Protestant backgrounds, reflecting their various places of origin in multiple German states, each having an established church. As a general rule throughout the United States, German Catholics and Protestants rarely settled within the same rural community, a pattern reflected in Central Texas.[65] Germans introduced Catholicism to rural

McLennan County, and Czech immigrants contributed to its spread. In the northeastern quadrant of the county, from 1870 to 1874, German Catholics established farms on the prairies surrounding a cotton gin community they initially named Martinsville, and later, Tours. One family hosted Catholic worship services in their home, led by the first resident priest of the newly organized Assumption Parish in Waco. Scattered families drove their wagons for miles for Catholic services, carrying their own benches for seating. Joining the Germans were a few Irish families also homesteading in the area. During Holy Week of 1874, the Catholics erected a small log church, completing it in time for Easter services and naming it St. Martin's. Mission priests from Waco, Marlin, and Fayetteville alternated biweekly trips to serve the church until 1888, when Rev. John Adelaar became St. Martin's first resident priest.[66]

When Adelaar arrived, he discovered a congregation in transition. During the 1880s and continuing for several decades, families of Czech descent filled in the prairies north and west of Tours, extending into Hill County. The Czechs, who migrated from earlier settlements in south Central Texas or directly from Bohemia and Moravia, worshipped among the German Americans at St. Martin's and gradually outnumbered them. The 1890 church census recorded sixty Czech, thirty German, and five Irish families. When St. Martin's opened a free parochial school in 1890 with classes provided in the German language for all students, the Czech families petitioned for their own parish. In 1893, they dedicated the Church of the Assumption of the Blessed Virgin Mary in the burgeoning rail town of West and initially shared a priest with St. Martin's. Assumption Parish grew large, eventually including Czech Catholic congregations in Abbott and Penelope in Hill County. West became Central Texas's primary center for Czech culture and social life.[67]

In the mid-1880s, Czech families spread into the community of Elk, about twelve miles south of Tours. Their numbers grew rapidly, and soon they outnumbered longtime Anglo families in the community. In the early 1900s, Elk residents formed a chapter of the Texas-based life insurance fraternal order, Slovanska Podporujici Jednota Statu Texas (SPJST), which operated, for the next ninety years, a dance hall featuring bands and orchestras specializing in polka and western swing music. Eventually, Czechs owned the town's stores and cotton gin. Beginning in 1922, Elk Catholics met in homes and celebrated mass once a month with a visiting priest from Waco. For worship on other Sundays, they traveled into Waco, weather permitting. In 1926, Elk Catholics dedicated their first church structure to St. Joseph, with sisters from Waco teaching catechism classes. At Easter, the Czech priest from West came to hear confessions from older members of the community in their native language. St. Joseph's at Elk remained a mission church, transferred in 1942 from Assumption parish in Waco to St. Martin's in Tours.[68]

Through the 1870s and 1880s, German Protestant families moved onto the black prairie and post oak country east of the Brazos River on either side of the McLennan-Falls County line. In 1872, Methodist circuit rider Ferdinand Mumme met with four German settlers and organized the Salem Society of the Methodist Episcopal Church. Within a year, sixteen German-speaking people gathered for twice-monthly services. Their numbers increased after Fritz von Schlumbach, who bought land in the vicinity in 1873, returned from a trip to Germany with about twenty-five people, mostly young men. In 1876, the growing congregation built its first building on Sandy Creek, and only nine years later, in 1885, built a larger building, which still served the congregation in 2001. In 1894, Salem Society hung a bell, which summoned worshippers on Sunday mornings and rang vespers on Saturday evenings. From Salem Society, later called Perry United Methodist Church, new German-speaking Methodist congregations developed: Meier Settlement in McLennan County, organized in 1887; Marlin, which had a brief life, from 1905 to 1915; and Meyers Memorial Church in Riesel, organized in 1914 and later renamed Riesel United Methodist Church.[69]

Ten years after the founding of Salem Society, increasing numbers of Germans farmed on either side of the Falls-McLennan County line between the rail stops at Riesel and Perry. On a Thursday, in December 1882, missionary John J. Trinklein of the Southern District of the Lutheran Church-Missouri Synod (LCMS) stepped off the train in Perry and began an immediate search for German families in the area to invite to Lutheran services. On the following Sunday, more than fifty people gathered in the home of George and Sarah Ebner, northeast of Perry, and the groundwork began for the establishment the next spring of Trinity Evangelical Lutheran Church at Friedens Au (prairie of peace, or peaceful meadow).[70] From the time of its founding on the Blackland Prairie, Trinity Lutheran occupied open land, with only its own school, parsonage, teacherage, and cemetery as neighbors. Beginning in 1898, the Trinity bell rang each Saturday evening, tolling vespers to remind listeners to prepare for the upcoming Lord's Day, and on Sunday morning, calling the church members to worship. Upon the death of a member, the bell tolled once for each year the person lived. By 1906, Trinity Lutheran was the fourth largest LCMS congregation in Texas. The church's membership peaked in the late 1930s–early 1940s, with 630 baptized and 440 communicant members. Only three pastors served the church over its first sixty-three years, from 1883 to 1946, providing stability unmatched by other Central Texas open-country churches.[71]

In 1880, the growth of German settlements in Texas attracted the attention of the Evangelical Synod of North America, a loosely organized denomination created in 1872 by Germans in the midwestern United States and a precursor to the current United Church of Christ. The next year Friederich Werning of Berger, Missouri, accepted the challenge of organizing Evangelical churches among Texas Germans. Because of its central location, Werning chose for his base the city of Waco, where he organized Zion Evangelical Church. From Waco he traced the route of railroads as they extended north and south, opening churches wherever he went. By 1888, ten Evangelical preachers served sixteen congregations in Texas, and a separate Texas District formed within the synod. In his memoirs, Werning confessed that many of the Evangelical missionaries who came south to aid his work failed to understand the nature of the cotton culture. Distance and climate discouraged some of them, and communities rose and fell with such rapidity that new congregations often disappeared within a year of their formation.[72] In Central Texas, nevertheless, German Evangelical congregations formed at West (St. Peter's, 1882); Robinson (St. John, 1884); Cego (St. Paul's, 1884); Otto (St. John's, 1886); Womack (Zion, 1891); Marlin (St. Paul, 1894); Gerald (St. Paul's, 1900); and Riesel (Friedens, 1904). In 1934, the Evangelical Synod of North America merged with the Reformed Church in the United States, creating the Evangelical and Reformed Church (E&R).[73]

Among the immigrant farmers moving to Central Texas in the second half of the nineteenth century were families from Washington County, Texas, who belonged to the German Baptist Conference, a national denomination organized in Pennsylvania in the 1840s. By 1884, Texas had four churches with 179 members that affiliated with both the northern group and the [Texas] Baptist State Convention, which in turn aligned with the Southern Baptist Convention.[74] Some of the families migrated to Cottonwood, just over the McLennan-Falls County line near Lorena, where they organized a German Baptist church. Others moved onto the prairies, one group locating west of Gatesville in Coryell County and another, in the corner formed where McLennan, Bosque, and Coryell Counties meet. Through the 1880s, the two groups gathered in homes, then schoolhouses, under the preaching of Julius Sydow, who alternated Sundays in each location, twenty-five miles apart. During the early 1890s, they organized separate churches—Bethel Heights (Coryell County, 1891) and Canaan (McLennan County, 1893)—and entered into fellowship with the German Baptist Conference.[75]

The founding of Canaan Baptist Church began with the 1885 migration of Heinrich and Wilhelmine Engelbrecht from Cedar Hill in Washington County to the prairies west of Crawford. The Engelbrechts sold two farms in Washington County for three and four times what land cost in northwestern McLennan County, enabling them to purchase sixteen hundred acres of prairie. Other Cedar Hill families joined the Engelbrechts, some beginning as their renters, and they all wrote to relatives remaining in Europe and invited them to Texas. Young men, especially, came and worked for the Engelbrechts, and six of them married their daughters. When the Engelbrechts moved from Washington County by train to Crawford, they carried with them thirty-five beehives. A few years later, because of the abundance of milk and honey about them, the church founders chose the name Canaan, based on biblical descriptions of the ancient land of the Israelites. At first, the farmers met for worship in homes, then in a schoolhouse, with Sydow preaching every other Sunday. The group bought a book of sermons, which Heinrich Engelbrecht and other men read on those Sundays when the preacher was at Bethel Heights church. In 1893, Canaan called its first full-time pastor, and in January 1895, Heinrich Engelbrecht donated land to the church for a building, parsonage, and cemetery. The only other community structure in the area of Canaan church was Prairie Chapel School, which in 1927 consolidated with Crawford schools and finally closed in 1939.[76]

The last major ethnic group that immigrated to Central Texas farmlands came the shortest distance. In Mexico, in 1900, 80 percent of the population was rural. The hacienda system and debt peonage kept most rural Mexicans in dire poverty and eventually forced them to leave. Under the regime of Porfirio Diaz (1886–1911), the Mexican government carried out various methods of eradicating small family farms. Up to five million families lost rights to their land.[77] Before 1910, some of these Mexican farmers came into north Central Texas in small groups or as individuals, working as migratory laborers. After the Mexican Revolution of 1910 spurred migration across the northern border, Central Texans recruited a significant number to aid their cotton harvests.[78] The

Mexican population of McLennan County rose from one hundred in 1900 to 4,100 in 1930, as Mexican citizens began settling as permanent residents. Most were agricultural workers, taking jobs as day laborers on farms or ranches. They maintained their language, and they also retained strong familial attachments with relatives in their homeland.

In 1924, missionaries from Spain's Franciscan order, the group that originated missions in colonial Texas, returned to the state to take charge of Catholic Mexican mission efforts. They chose Waco as their headquarters, and on their way there they visited a small Catholic chapel built before World War I by Mexican farm workers outside the community of Satin, west of the Brazos River in Falls County. Building on land reportedly donated by a German family, the Mexican laborers named their chapel Santa Rita, for Rita of Cascia, canonized in 1900 as the saint of desperate causes. In Waco, the Franciscans established St. Francis on the Brazos church and parish and then turned their attention to organizing Mexican Catholics in small rail towns throughout Central Texas. St. Rita's appears to be the region's earliest Mexican Catholic congregation and the only one established in open country.[79]

Founded on faith in God by families who for generations past had farmed the land, the churches described above faced profound challenges during the twentieth century. The nature of Texas agriculture changed dramatically, causing remarkable loss of rural population. By 1930, in McLennan County, more people (53.5 percent) lived in Waco than in open country, cotton-gin villages, or rail towns.[80] One cause of rural depopulation was the cycle of poverty created by the crop-lien system. By 1930, almost three-quarters of McLennan County farmers worked land owned by someone else, and the majority of farm families spent their days in want. The crop-lien system became institutionalized as the demand for cotton acreage surpassed its availability, causing land prices to skyrocket. Rising prices in turn consolidated ownership in the hands of the few. The crop-lien system, which generated little loyalty between landowners and tenants, meant that communities were always in flux. Sharecroppers and tenants moved every two or three years, hoping for larger crops and better treatment. With the shift of cotton to the plains and with increased mechanization, longtime farmers sold large tracts of land, displacing dozens of tenant and sharecropping families overnight.[81]

As agricultural change began pushing people away from the farm, the city began pulling young people toward a new life. Affordable automobiles and improved roads provided the means of exit. Until they bought their first Model T Fords, most farm people lived in circumscribed worlds, going only as far as they could reach on horseback or by mule-drawn wagon and still return home in time to feed the livestock. By 1930, however, people living on farms or in small towns owned 42 percent of the nation's vehicles.[82] The automobile required improved roads, and in McLennan County, in 1911, the first gravel road was laid between McGregor and South Bosque, followed in two years by the first asphalt road, between Waco and Lorena. Rural roads remained mostly gravel until after World War II, when funds became available to surface farm-to-market roads across Texas. McLennan County claimed to be the first Central Texas county to hard surface all its rural routes.[83]

Even as Texas prided itself for the construction of good roads, the state ranked low in public education, with much of the blame falling upon the proliferation of one-room country schools. In 1904, education reformers termed country schools "truly wretched," citing inexperienced, undereducated teachers and poor buildings and equipment. The lack of high schools in rural areas required farm and ranch families wanting their children to continue past the primary level to arrange boarding for them in town. Beginning in 1893, the Texas legislature passed a series of laws enabling consolidation of schools, and over the next several decades, improved roads allowed students to travel from closed one-room schools to larger primary schools and to high schools in the nearest small towns. In McLennan County, in 1912, Ross became the first centralized district to employ transportation for its rural students, using two horse-drawn hacks with a capacity of about twenty-five children each. Nine years later, a single Ford truck replaced the wagons. In 1927, the McLennan County school board trustees centralized twenty-four rural school districts into six towns, and by 1930, thirty-seven buses carried 1,073 pupils to schools in sixteen rural districts. Also by that year, the number of county schools located outside independent school districts decreased to forty-five, from 107 in 1923.[84] The trend toward school consolidation increased statewide with the passage of the Gilmer-Aiken laws in 1949, and in McLennan County, successive mergers spelled the end of the country school.

Better transportation and centralized schools came in conjunction with the failure of the crop-lien system and the transition from a credit to cash economy, all of which contributed to the demise of the general store at Central Texas crossroads.[85] With increased accessibility to town shopping and entertainment, rural people also found it easier to commute into the city for work. The process of urbanization in McLennan County exploded during World War I. The openings of Camp MacArthur and Rich Field in Waco and the subsequent growth of support services for the military bases provided employment outside farming. In the 1920s, severe droughts forced farm families to look for alternative living situations, and answers came with the appearance of manufacturing operations in Waco and its environs. Those first leaving farming were the young people coming of age to earn their own livings.

The Central Texas economy further diversified in the 1930s and 1940s. New Deal programs introduced crop reductions, price supports, federal credit agencies, and soil conservation. Agricultural reforms intensified the push of tenants off the land and into jobs in town. Cotton production moved west and southwest, as mechanical irrigation brought life to the arid plains. With the crop went its ancillary businesses, and gradually all but one of McLennan County's seventy-five cotton gins closed or moved west.[86] With cotton's decline, livestock and livestock products increased. In the 1940s, farm youth enlisted in military service or took jobs in wartime industries. Mechanization replaced human labor, large-scale farming and ranching operations replaced family farms, and growing towns swallowed the closest rural settlements.

By the end of World War II, 65 percent of McLennan County residents lived in Waco.[87] The city drew people away from farms in surrounding counties as well as McLennan County. Following the trend in neighboring counties, Bosque County farms became fewer in number and larger in size. The shallow Grand Prairie soils, weakened by a succession of exhaustive droughts, eroded away in the floods that followed. In Falls County, the Great Depression brought a 64 percent decrease in farms, with their value dropping by 55 percent. During World War II, the U.S. Army annexed approximately 225 square miles of Coryell County to create Camp Hood, decimating twenty-four communities and nearly twelve hundred farms. In subsequent decades, farming fell to less than 8 percent of the county's income. Employment at the military base and large units of the Texas Department of Corrections replaced agricultural jobs and supplemented the incomes of families who stayed on the land to raise cattle and feed.[88]

These demographic shifts had profound impacts on rural churches, most of which did not survive the changes. Memberships of some churches that originated in open country merged with town congregations. Parent denominations often encouraged consolidation of congregations with small numbers and sold the rural church property. In that manner, six of seven McLennan County Methodist churches founded by Anglos in open country gradually closed over the following decades. A spreading suburb engulfed Spring Valley Methodist, the lone survivor.[89]

As the people left the countryside, former communities dried up. Other villages and their churches shared the fate of Battle, in eastern McLennan County. Formed in 1880, Battle had Methodist, Baptist, and Lutheran churches, a school, and a general store to serve the surrounding neighborhood, occupied mostly by stock raisers. In 1902, the railroad from Marlin passed through Battle, but a few miles east along the lines a new town developed and prospered at Mart. In 1927, Battle school consolidated with Mart. Fire destroyed both the Baptist and Methodists churches, which were never rebuilt. By 1940, the Lutheran Church-Missouri Synod phased out the Battle congregation in favor of Grace Lutheran, Mart.[90] This pattern repeated all over Central Texas, as villages lost people and churches closed.

A few village churches survived the loss of their surrounding communities through absorption into developing Waco suburbs. In South Bosque, for example, successive floods convinced most businesses to vacate the community by the end of World War I. In 1929, a cement plant began operation a few miles east, and many area fathers and sons found steady work there and left farming. After World War II, the remaining cotton gin was sold to a buyer who dismantled it and moved it to West Texas. The school consolidated with Hewitt and Speegleville schools in 1947. The widening of Highway 84 and expansion of Lake Waco caused the few remaining families to move their houses away from the original South Bosque site, which lived on only in the memories of older people. The Harris Creek Church remained an active Baptist-Methodist union congregation until 1960, when the Methodists combined with Woodway United Methodist Church in an adjacent bedroom community.[91] The Baptists remained at Harris Creek, and new housing developments in the area multiplied their numbers. From 1990 to 1999 the church's membership increased 172 percent.[92] Similar transformation of one-time villages to populous suburbs aided the persistence of other churches throughout Central Texas.

What, then, is the nature of Central Texas rural life in the early twenty-first century? Although depopulation caused the loss of farm communities, agriculture remained extremely important in the region. In 1997, McLennan County appeared in the list of one hundred leading agricultural counties in the United States, with 2,006 farms.[93] Agricultural success, however, was no longer the story of the individual family, bound together with neighbors through the local school and church. Fewer people grew a greater diversity of crops and livestock on increasingly more expensive land. Many small farmers, forced out by low commodity prices, sold out to agricultural corporations or to city folk seeking land for recreational purposes. Development of rural water systems made country living more appealing for commuters with city jobs, and acres of farmland were divided into home sites. Many of the remaining farms not owned by corporations were part-time ones, operated by people with steady incomes elsewhere who kept a few head of cattle or raised hay to maintain agricultural activity on their country acreage.[94]

Change is obvious and explainable on the rural landscape. More remarkable is that here and there are signs of continuity symbolized by the persistence of churches built in open country during cotton's dominion. How and why have these congregations survived? Through oral history research with representative congregations, Central Texans voiced the following answers to questions about the longevity of their churches: continuity of the founding families; remembrance of ethnic origins; sense of place, associated with one's social, personal, and spiritual formation; and adaptation to change.

CHAPTER 2

Belonging to the Family

"THE FELLOWSHIP OF KINDRED MINDS IS LIKE TO THAT ABOVE."

—*Blest Be the Tie*

AT THE OPENING OF THE twenty-first century, most worshippers who gathered on Sunday mornings in Central Texas open-country churches were descendants of those who organized and consecrated these sacred spaces on the prairie in the late nineteenth and early twentieth centuries. Donald Julius Richter's grandfather was a founding member of St. Paul's United Church of Christ at Gerald in 1900. Through the years, so many members of his extended family belonged to the former German Evangelical and Reformed church in northeastern McLennan County that Richter said, "To me, St. Paul's and my family has all been about the same thing. The family has always been involved in the church together." Alice Margaret Miller, born in 1938, was kin to all the major families except one in St. Paul United Church of Christ in the Cego community in western Falls County. She reported, "It means a lot to me to know that this is where my family, my great-grandfather, came to and settled, and then his children and all have lived there for years and helped build the church and were a part of the church."[1]

STEEPLE, MOUNT MORIAH BAPTIST CHURCH, RIESEL

Many rural churches began essentially as family chapels, encompassing large extended kinship groups and close neighbors, interrelated by marriage. Oris Pierson, from rural Bosque County, confessed that he "became a Lutheran because my parents were Lutherans. And my parents were Lutherans, I know, because their parents were. But in the growing up process, I've found no reason why I should try to find some other place where I wanted to worship. It became a kind of a feeling of satisfaction to me and still is." Likewise, B. F. Engelbrecht, from western McLennan County, stated that at Canaan Baptist Church, first organized around his grandparents' kitchen table, the membership constituted "nearly a circle," because, he explained, "nearly everybody's kin some way. It's just a big family."[2]

When young people abandoned rural life for urban jobs and conveniences, some maintained family connections that drew them back to the country church on Sundays. In the early years of the twentieth century, Fannie Cook Brown lived in

Gatesville, county seat of Coryell County, where she raised fourteen children, but weather and health permitting, on second and fourth Sundays she walked with her children back to her home community of Lincolnville. There, in the countryside, they spent the day in Bethlehem Baptist Church with dozens of aunts, uncles, and cousins. Her youngest daughter, Eunice Johnson, born in 1897, recalled spending all day at church, with three services—morning, "evening," and night—and dinner on the grounds. Fannie Brown and her female relatives prepared baskets of food to share around tables set up outdoors on the church grounds for the mid-day meal. As the long day progressed, with services continuing past sundown, mothers spread quilts on the church floor so the babies and young children could sleep.[3]

Typical of hundreds of other rural Central Texas youth in the 1940s, Ima Hoppe Bekkelund moved into Waco upon completing high school, leaving her parents' farm to find work packing bottles at the Owens-Illinois glass plant. Her move into the city had little impact, however, on her faithful attendance at Canaan Baptist Church. During the five years she worked at the glass plant, on weekends she did not work, she rode the bus to McGregor, where a family member met her and drove her home to the farm to visit her family and attend church on Sunday. Thus began a tradition that continued after her marriage and lasted for more than fifty years: commuting from Waco, and later suburban Woodway, to attend Sunday services at Canaan Baptist Church. A prime motivation for Ima Bekkelund's Sunday treks to the country was the traditional afternoon family gathering at the site of her parents' farm. "I was born on that same place and I'm still going to that same place," she explained. "And now my mother and father are gone, but my nephew bought part of the place and he's built a new home there. So we have a big gathering every Sunday in our nephew's home. We just love it out in the country."[4]

By the end of the twentieth century, more members of Springhill United Methodist Church, in eastern McLennan County, lived in the city than in the country, but the church's membership remained fairly stable. Typical of Springhill members was Glenda Gala Garrett, who as a teenager in the late 1960s left her father's farm to live in Waco, leaving behind a large family network whose roots in the area extended back a century. Garrett enjoyed the economic and social advantages of city life, but in her experience, the city church had "so many members till you can't really be individualized, whereas in the rural church you have your own individual Christianity." Second and fourth Sundays, when Springhill held worship services, Garrett drove to the country for church, taking along her city-raised son and grandchildren. Her motivation, she explained, was family, in both a real and a spiritual sense. "You can come to church, you can feel that warmth, that welcome, that love. You are welcome because you are a child of God. So not just because I was born and raised there and my family was originated there and they were some of the beginners of Springhill, my soul is a part of Springhill."[5]

The continuing influence of the ancestors in the remaining open-country churches becomes evident to the stranger through commemorative plaques in the foyers, memorial citations hung on walls, photographs of past leaders, nameplates on pews, and among the silent markers in the adjoining cemeteries. For Louise Yows, St. John Lutheran Church at Coryell City was "a comfort zone," because, she noted, "all of our family is still in the church or out here in the cemetery, and so it's home." At Canaan Baptist Church, where the church doors open eastward to a view of the well-manicured cemetery, Pastor Robert Scott found it "meaningful and spiritual" to remind the congregation, "Your ancestors, some of whom are buried out there, planted a seed of faith. Today we are reaping the harvest." Former German Evangelical and Reformed (E&R) congregations in open country in Falls and McLennan Counties likewise have cemeteries nearby, where both family and ethnic heritage remain strongly evident. Faced with aging, diminishing memberships, several of these churches, now aligned with the United Church of Christ, resist merging with larger related congregations in Riesel, Robinson, and Waco. Lorraine Kluge, the widow of a longtime E&R pastor, explained, "When the churches have a cemetery, they don't want to give up easily. That's something that you want to hang on to."[6]

At Springhill United Methodist Church, the drive from the road to the church winds through the graveyard, a poignant reminder of generations past. Pastor Carol Grant Gibson described the strong symbolic presence of "family past" among her members: "There is a cemetery that's next to the church, and their relatives, parents, grandparents, many of them are buried on that property. And they're just enveloped by home. Many of them grew up out there, even though they moved into town. And so they have a real sense of ownership and pride in that church and a determination to see it continue as best they can." In 1969, Springhill member Arlelia Glasker Garrett initiated a memorial fund that through the years allowed practical and aesthetic additions to the sanctuary and church grounds, all duly registered in annual homecoming books. Items purchased in memory of deceased loved ones ranged from new altar ware, pulpit parament, and sanctuary flowers to improved parking areas, a storage building, and a cemetery entrance arch.[7]

Strong family ties helped many young adults retain interest in their parents' rural church. Father Isidore Rozychi explained that the descendants of the core families that in the 1920s started St. Joseph's Catholic Church at Elk, in eastern McLennan County, "still form the heart and nucleus of that area." In the church's seventy-seventh year, Father Rozychi claimed, "We have six or seven that are really young that are bringing in new life, new ideas. They're keeping their name, the tradition, their heritage. They're preserving it." Loyalty to the home parish, however, transcended the miles for many of those who left Elk area farms and ranches upon completing their education, marrying, and taking urban jobs. Father Rozychi went so far as to credit the persistence of St. Joseph's Church to the middle-aged generation that lived up to three hours away but still returned on weekends to visit older family members. On their return trips, they brought their children to worship in the parish church where they themselves were baptized, perpetuating, Rozychi said, the "pride" and "good memories" of the religious center that had served their family for three-quarters of a century.[8]

In addition to occasional attendance, the congregation in absentia sent financial support to the old home church. St. Paul's United Church of Christ, Gerald, celebrated its one-hundredth anniversary in 2000 largely because of past support from generations living elsewhere. In the winter of 1978, a fire, which began in old wiring, destroyed St. Paul's parish hall, built in 1932 with funds raised by the Ladies Aid. The fire also took the Sunday-school annex, constructed in 1956 between the sanctuary and parish hall. The annex symbolized a community memory, because the congregation constructed it with lumber from the old Gerald School, which closed in 1948. So with the loss of the church annex and parish hall, the surrounding community also lost the last physical evidence of its former school building. Fortunately, the fire spared the forty-year-old sanctuary. Albert Henry Leuschner remembered that the congregation hesitated briefly before rebuilding: "When the ashes were there, you know, people did talk about, Well, maybe we should forget it." Raising funds for rebuilding seemed an insurmountable task until money began arriving from the widely scattered descendants of Gerald's longtime families. With financial help from its extended family and community friends, St. Paul's enlarged its parish hall and Sunday-school space and modernized its worship center.[9]

J. J. ASLEEP, SPRINGHILL UNITED METHODIST CHURCH, RIESEL

The Birome Church, just over the McLennan County line in southeastern Hill County, relied on one-day annual homecomings to meet its year-round financial needs. Pastor William Gardiner Ellis indicated that family identity inspired generous homecoming offerings. "These people like to meet these people in the community. They intermarried. They lived there." At homecomings, Ellis heard them boast, "This is Grandma over here. This is my granddaughter over here." Birome began as a church of tenant farm families, primarily working land on the Cartwright Ranch. Many of the children who grew up picking cotton on their parents' shares served in World War II, left farming, and entered other trades and professions. Once, according to Ellis, "these people were the folks that couldn't ride to Leroy because they couldn't pay the price," but photos of recent Birome Church homecomings indicated their arrivals in luxury automobiles. One Sunday a year, in July, church attendance increased tenfold as former members reconvened in Birome, sharing memories, worship, and lunch, and bringing their offerings. According to Garnet L. Vardeman, people like him, who returned for homecoming, recognized their role in the church's upkeep. "I think they give generously," Vardeman explained, "because they want to see the church perpetuating." A church sustained by family sentiment needs an active resident membership to survive, however. In 2001, as its regular membership declined below a dozen and its minister passed his ninety-second birthday, the former Baptist-Methodist union church at Birome closed its doors.[10]

Lifelong affection toward a country church is traceable to experiences in early childhood, when a youngster was among family at church as well as at home. A year before Birome Church closed, Margaret Norman Smith reflected on its lasting influences on her life, stating, "It is a good foundation for our lives, socially and spiritually, and we wouldn't have been the same without it." Growing up in small, open-country churches, surrounded by kin and neighbors, children felt secure within known boundaries. Grandparents, aunts, uncles, older cousins, choir members, deacons, ushers, and pastors, in addition to parents, all took interest in a child's behavior. Before World War II, in many rural churches, families separated by gender and age when taking their seats in church on Sundays. At St. Paul's Evangelical and Reformed Church, Cego, women sat on the west side and men on the east side. Children sat with their mothers, sometimes falling asleep in their laps. At St. Joseph's Catholic Church, Elk, men and women sat on opposite sides and children occupied the front row, girls on the women's side and boys on the men's side. Rosalee Smajstrla Urbis recalled, "When you got old enough not to be in Mama's arms and you could behave, you could sit on that front seat." With the whole congregation watching, discipline was swift. Walter Dulock remembered that at St. Joseph's, "If you misbehaved in church and you got home, you knew you was going to get a good lecture and a good whipping. You made that mistake one time; you didn't make that mistake a second time."[11]

Likewise, children in worship services at Springhill Methodist Church knew that their misdeeds in church were subject to correction by anyone present. Glenda Garrett recalled that when she was a child in the 1950s, a certain look, a thump on the head, a tug of the ear, or a quick pinch told a fidgeting or whispering child, "Look, settle down." Garrett believed such community discipline provided security for youngsters because it expanded their sense of family and belonging. "It takes everybody in the church as well as in the community," Garrett said, "to keep Springhill what it's always been. So I'm still one that if I see someone's child do wrong, I'm going to tell them, and then I'll tell the parent what I did. We all have to look out for each other."[12]

Before World War II, as children grew into adolescence, they felt pressure to remain faithful in attending Sunday services at the family church. Within the Czech community, Saturday nights brought music and dancing to the local fraternal hall. For young people, the weekly dance was the only available social event for meeting the opposite sex and courting someone special. Mary Hanak met John Simcik, her future husband, at just such a dance. As socially important as the dances were, however, mothers warned their sons and daughters that their late-night fun did not lessen the expectation that they would be in place at church the next day. "Sleepy or not sleepy, Sunday morning you go to church, believe you me. That was a must," Mary Simcik recalled. The long-ingrained habit stayed with her; for forty-five years following the birth of her youngest son, Simcik claimed, she missed only one Sunday in church.[13]

For many young people growing up in rural families in the early twentieth century, spiritual direction at home complemented religious training at church. Christian parents planted seeds of faith in their children's souls through example and instruction. Bessie Lee Stafford, lifelong member of Bethlehem Baptist Church, reported that her mother, Mary Ann Mayberry Barrens, made spiritual matters "one of the main topics of conversation" in her country home in Coryell County. "My mother was very religious," Stafford remembered, "and we didn't have to have an alarm clock to wake us up in the morning because she prayed every morning. That was her first duty." Likewise, Bettie Mayberry Weatherly, born in 1878, one of nineteen children of former slave James Mayberry, founder of Bethlehem Baptist Church, used the quiet times in the evening after work for instructing her five daughters. One daughter, Rowena Weatherly Keatts, recalled, "We had a fireplace, and we'd sit down around that fireplace. Well, my daddy would sit there too, but he'd soon go to bed. But my mother would sit there and she would talk with us. She would tell us of the evils of the world. She would ask us to read to her certain scriptures. She was a firm believer in God and she

LEAVING CHURCH, SPRINGHILL UNITED METHODIST CHURCH, RIESEL

prayed." Keatts said that Bettie Weatherly prayed every night on her knees with her children. She taught them to recite the Lord's Prayer, and when they forgot the words, she told them to pray simply, "Lord, have mercy on me." Scripture reading and prayers "just grew up in all of us," Rowena Keatts said, and in adulthood she and her sisters maintained the devotional life learned by their mother's example.[14]

With their parents as models, successive generations learned to be faithful stewards of their religious heritage. The spiritual legacy of former slave George Glasker, one of the earliest members of Springhill Methodist Church, extended by the end of the twentieth century into the sixth generation. Along with the families related to them by marriage, Glasker descendants helped keep Springhill Methodist alive and active, and over the years two felt a call to ministry and became pastors. One descendant, Elizabeth Glasker, served Springhill as communion stewardess and prayer service leader. Her daughter, Arlelia Glasker Garrett, served the church as recording secretary, president of the United Methodist Women, communion stewardess, choir member, and certified lay mission speaker for the district conference. For many years before her death, Arlelia Garrett was also the church's historian, and her daughter Glenda Garrett succeeded her in that position. Another of Arlelia Garrett's daughters, Ernestine Garrett Anderson, achieved her nursing degree and for over twenty years traveled the world with her husband during his years of military service. Upon retirement, Ernestine and Charles Anderson returned to build a new home adjacent to land belonging to her father, Booker T. Garrett, a site just down the road and around the curve from Springhill church. Following in the footsteps of her maternal ancestors, Ernestine Anderson plunged into service at her childhood church because, she explained, "one of my forefathers was a founder of this church, and so I feel a need to do my part in my generation as they did in theirs, because they paved the way for us." She became pianist and music leader and served as the church's recording secretary and as officer for the United Methodist Women. She was the assistant to the adult Sunday-school teacher, who was her husband, Charles. Ernestine Anderson also created the church bulletins and homecoming booklets. She led a prayer band and served twenty years as coordinator for the United Methodist Youth. In keeping with family tradition, the Andersons' two adult children maintained memberships in Springhill and sent their tithes to the home church although they lived and worked in Dallas and Fort Worth.[15]

Similar stories abounded among the descendants of rural German Protestants, whose family legacy of service to their churches abided through several generations. One of Alice Miller's earliest childhood memories, from the early 1940s, was "laying on the hard bench and sleeping with my head in my mama's lap" at St. Paul's Evangelical and Reformed Church, Cego. She reported, "Mom and Dad didn't send me. My mom and dad took me to church, took all of us." Her father, Albert Miller, was longtime Sunday-school secretary and teacher in the church, built on land donated by his uncle. Although Alice Miller's mother "was a quiet person, not an outgoing person," she taught Sunday school "for years and years and years." Church was where Alice Miller and her siblings, cousins, aunts, and uncles gathered for picnics, Christmas programs, Easter egg hunts, and baseball games. In adulthood, she served on the church council and, for more than thirty years, was treasurer of the North Texas Association of the South Central Conference of the United Church of Christ. Like her aunt, Flora Huber, before her, Alice Miller served as church pianist.[16]

Almost always, deacons at Canaan Baptist Church were descendants of the German families who founded the church in 1893. Jerry Gauer was a fourth-generation deacon at Canaan, and he held hopes that his sons would follow in his footsteps. Besides being a deacon at Canaan, Jerry Gauer served as Sunday-school secretary, trustee, and caretaker for the church's perpetual care cemetery. Van Doren Massirer, a farmer on Canaan Church Road, left the church of his childhood when he became an adult and married his non-German, non-Baptist sweetheart. His mother remained active at Canaan Baptist into her nineties, however, and Massirer observed that "a core of the original families out here are the ones that keep it going. They're devout people who are there every Sunday." Besides supporting the church financially, they "look after things," Massirer reported, including taking care of the buildings and cemetery. Speaking of the family heritage, he said, "I think that's the heart and soul of this church up here."[17]

Woven together with family continuity, threads of cultural heritage contributed to the endurance of open-country churches. Along country back roads, Christians of different ethnic and racial backgrounds withdrew into separate churches on Sunday mornings, long past assimilation in other spheres of life. More than fifty years after Norwegians first settled in Bosque County, their Lutheran churches continued to discourage acculturation and assimilation among their people, according to Oris Pierson. Born in 1899 to Norwegian parents on a farm west of Clifton, Pierson

reached adolescence, he said, before he realized, "We were peculiar to other people because we made ourselves that way." For the Norwegians, the distinction was clear: "Anybody that was not a Norwegian was an American, and the line was drawn." All Americans were "taboo," Pierson remembered, and fell short of the character strengths the Norwegians attributed to themselves, including hard work, generosity, and sound money management. The local minister served only the

Norwegian community, to the extent, Pierson claimed, "he didn't go out of his way even to invite anybody else." Assimilation began soon after the turn of the twentieth century among children, like Oris Pierson, who upon entering school acquired English and learned to work, study, and play with non-Norwegian children. The church influenced the community in one positive way that smoothed the path to assimilation later, Pierson noted. Because the churches were self-sufficient, their members earned reputations as "good, honest, hard-working people who had something to offer and who had something to give to somebody else." The church's strong influence on its members, particularly upon the behavior of its young people, aided the construction of an identity of wholesomeness within the Norwegian community. Pierson and his Norwegian friends gradually came to realize that "there were a lot of good to everybody else if we'd only look for it." As his generation grew into adulthood, some married outside the Norwegian community, and intermarriage among their German and Anglo neighbors strengthened mutual understanding. By 1972, Oris Pierson could say, "Now you don't know who's Norwegian and who isn't around here."[18]

German Americans in rural Central Texas shared with Norwegian Americans elements of distinctiveness from the majority culture. Born in 1936, Van Doren Massirer perceived among his German American relatives in Canaan Baptist Church a "general disdain" for "the other people, the non-Germans," whose fields and houses did not reflect their own "spit and polish" work ethic. Among themselves, Massirer's family used as a benchmark of good farming the straightness of hand-tilled crop rows. "You can rest assured," he said, "that those who didn't do their job quite as well got talked about."[19]

Some German churches maintained their distinctiveness proudly. Many displayed their ethnicity in the architecture and design of the church. In 1909, the members of St. Paul's Evangelical Church, Gerald, added an inscription, in German, to the wooden arch over the chancel, constructed with the first building in 1903. Painted in gold, the lettering displayed the biblical injunction: Seek first the kingdom of God. In 1937, the congregation erected a new, larger building, the one that still stands today, and carpenters added wood to the arch to extend it across the wider chancel. Over ninety years since its creation, the inscribed arch still announces to worshippers the German roots of the congregation.[20] Other rural Catholic, Evangelical and Reformed, and Lutheran congregations decorated their sanctuaries with colorful stained-glass windows, often containing German inscriptions.

Known among its neighbors in western Falls County as "the German church" at Cego, St. Paul's United Church of Christ reached its one-hundredth anniversary in 1984 having baptized in its history 423 persons and confirmed 217, all of German descent. According to the church's pastor, Jeffrey W. Taylor, members of St. Paul's had "a feeling of rootedness" within the solemn liturgical worship tradition of their originating denomination, the Evangelical Synod of North America. A Baptist neighbor of St. Paul's reported that solidarity among Cego's German families influenced them to blackball repeated attempts by her church to join the local Germania Mutual Insurance Company in order to participate in its fire insurance plan. Even in death, the distinct ethnic groups at Cego kept their distance, dividing the local cemetery between the German plots, placed on the lower part of the hill descending toward St. Paul's church, and the Anglo plots, situated higher on the hill in sight of the Baptist church.[21]

Differences advanced beyond exclusiveness when world events intervened. During the First World War, B. F. Engelbrecht recalled, his father came home to western McLennan County from doing business in town one day with news of rumors that the Americans were going to "chase every German family out of this community." The Engelbrechts' church, Canaan Baptist, experienced minor harassment from Anglo youths who disrupted creek-side baptisms by making remarks and throwing rocks. Their neighbors at St. John Lutheran Church, two miles away at Coryell City, however, faced a more direct anti-German challenge. "We had a Lutheran preacher up there, and he was still preaching German," B. F. Engelbecht reported, "and they went up there with horses and told him, If you don't get out of here by sunup in the morning, we'll kill you." Two daughters of the Lutheran pastor were teachers at Prairie Chapel School and boarded with the Engelbrecht family. Marvin Engelbrecht told his younger brother B. F. that he remembered that the teachers cried when their father came to the Engelbrecht home and told them they had to move immediately to a friendlier place.[22]

During World War II, Earlien Freyer Engelbrecht experienced firsthand some of the anti-German sentiments that divided neighbors in Texas communities with large German American populations. For the most part, people of various ethnicities "were kind and good and everybody got along so good together," she claimed. Yet, she added, "when the wars broke out, that's when the problem started." One day a government agent came to the Engelbrecht home to ask questions

MAJORS CHAPEL UNITED METHODIST CHURCH, NEAR GOLINDA

about Canaan Baptist's pastor, Cornelius C. Gossen. Raised a Mennonite, Gossen was a pacifist and refused to take up arms. Earlien Engelbrecht said, "I told them pretty quick what I thought about it. . . . I just told him, 'Our preacher's not a Nazi.' I said, 'He's a Christian man.'" In her pastor's defense, she told the agent, "'Just because he wouldn't bear arms, well, that's everybody's privilege.'" While government officials investigated their pastor, local vandals defaced the outdoor sign at Canaan Baptist, removing -an from the designation German Baptist Church.[23]

Language set apart congregations founded by immigrants from their Anglo neighbors, and, yielding to both external and internal pressures, most of the churches appropriated English into their worship program by the 1940s. The route taken by Canaan Baptist Church toward English-language services was typical of other German-language churches. Edna Jaeckle Dreyer, born in 1914, was the third generation of her family to attend Canaan Baptist, a tradition begun by her Austrian grandmother who became a charter member there in 1891. Dreyer's earliest recollection was the weekly ride to the one-room German Baptist church in her father's horse-drawn buggy. At Sunday school, children like Dreyer, who spoke only German at home until they began public school, learned the German alphabet and read from Bible storybooks written in German. Even though she understood the language of the worship service, the sermons still seemed long and hard to follow for Dreyer, who remembered, "the pastors made a long prayer and we had to stand up for the prayer, and that was kind of hard on the children." Families carried their own hymnals to church, and the Jaeckle family had three German-language songbooks to take every week, one each for Sunday school, morning worship, and evening worship. The Sunday-school literature came with the lessons written in both German and English.[24]

Like Edna Dreyer, Canaan member B. F. Engelbrecht, born in 1916, remembered that in his childhood, "We sang German, we prayed German, and we taught German." In addition to including German language lessons in Sunday school, the church sponsored a German school during the summer months to teach the youngsters to read, write, and sing in German. The blending of voices in German by Canaan's choir remained one of B. F. Engelbrecht's favorite memories. German music, he said, "has such an even flow when you sing it. It's just beautiful and I still love it." He demonstrated his affinity in later life during many annual Christmas Eve services when he and his wife, Earlien, performed "Silent Night" together in German. German services at church came easy

for B. F. Engelbrecht because, he said, "My folks never did talk English," only German. When his father, Henry W. Engelbrecht, went to Crawford or Waco on business, he enjoyed conversations with German Jewish shop owners, and when Jewish peddlers brought their wares into the country for trade, the Engelbrechts welcomed them in German. At age eighty, B. F. Engelbrecht could still recite the German blessing he had heard "twenty years at home three times a day": *Segne, Vater, diese*

Speise, Uns zur Kraft und Dir zum Preise [Bless, our Father, this our food, For Thy glory and our good].

By the 1930s, however, most of Canaan's youth spoke, wrote, and read English rather than German. In those days, Canaan had a large population of young people, with several related families having eight to ten children apiece. They gathered at choir practice on Friday nights, held parties on Saturday nights, and visited on Sunday afternoons between morning and evening church services. During the mid-1920s, Rev. George Hege had organized *Jugend Verein,* or Young People's Union, for children and young adults, ages ten through twenty-six. The popular program met every Sunday evening and included singing and Bible study conducted in German. B. F. Engelbrecht remembered that his older brothers and their cousins and friends encouraged Hege's successor, C. C. Gossen, to use English during their gatherings, and the church replaced *Jugend Verein* with Baptist Young People's Union (BYPU), using exclusively English-language Southern Baptist literature.

Gradually, Canaan converted its other programs from German to English. Following the switch to BYPU, the church began holding Sunday evening preaching services in English, as well. The change necessitated the purchase of new English songbooks. On New Year's Day in 1940 a majority of Canaan's members voted to go with English for all preaching and singing. B. F. Engelbrecht realized the difficulty the change presented for his parents, who "were shook up about it," he said, and his father, especially, "wasn't quite ready to do that," he added. Long after the transition to English, for as long as he continued to teach Canaan's adult women's Sunday-school class, B.F.'s father, Henry W. Engelbrecht presented the lessons in German.[25]

Czech immigrants dropped their native language more rapidly than many Germans. One motivation for rapid assimilation was to curtail prejudice. Czech Catholics at Elk experienced conflicts with Protestants before World War II when their school consolidated with Axtell, a predominantly Anglo community that required its teachers to attend the Baptist church on Sundays, regardless of their religious affiliation. Walter Dulock explained, "It looked like there was an imaginary line between the Baptist church and the Catholics." The Anglos called the Czechs "biscuit-eaters" or "mackerel-snappers" because they did not eat meat on Fridays. When Robert Cunningham began dating Evelyn Mae Smajstrla in 1945 and met her ten siblings, he learned, "their parents required that their children speak English and not Czech. Not that they didn't want them to know Czech, but they insisted, particularly the father, that their kids now lived in America and they wanted them to speak English." The Smajstrlas' desire for rapid assimilation was common among members of the Czech churches pastored by Isidore Rozychi. He noted, "The basic European customs and traditions were brought here and these people became Americanized. They kept a lot of their background culture, but still they let the American spirit come in to start a new tradition, a new heritage."[26]

By the time the second generation of immigrant descendants born in rural Texas grew into adulthood, their grandparents' native language was strange to them, improved transportation carried them beyond their ethnic neighborhood, and many found marriage partners outside their cultural and denominational group. Within German and Czech Catholic families, especially before World War II, dating and marriage outside the ethnic community induced tension, but even more disruptive than unions across ethnic lines were Catholic-Protestant ones. Mary Hanak and John Simcik's engagement in 1920 caused great consternation for their parents. Both young people were natives of Czechoslovakia whose families immigrated to McLennan County in the early 1900s, but different religious affiliations created a sharp division between their families. The Hanaks worshipped at St. Martin's at Tours and the Simciks worshipped at the Czech Moravian Brethren Church. More than fifty years later, Simcik recalled vividly that her mother called her fiancé "a lost sheep," while her future mother-in-law accused the Hanaks of idolatry because of the statues in their church. The young couple eventually eloped, married by a priest in Waco who agreed to perform the ceremony in the rectory, but not the church. They each continued in their separate denominations for the remainder of their lives.[27]

Ethnic distinctions fostered separatism but simultaneously promoted unity among culturally similar congregations miles apart. When Mexican farm workers built St. Rita's Catholic chapel near Satin in western Falls County in 1912, they raised funds for the building and to support visiting priests through fiestas. The annual December twelfth feast in honor of Our Lady of Guadalupe was especially popular, attracting Mexican American families from a twenty-mile radius in all directions. Those without wagons or horses walked the distance to celebrate the appearance of the Blessed Virgin in the form of a young Mexican woman. By 1924, when Waco's Franciscan missionaries needed funding to build the city's first Spanish-language Catholic church, they sought the help of Ernesto Chavez, who had organized the St. Rita's fiestas for years. Chavez, who by then lived in Waco, involved his entire family in preparations for fiestas held at St. Rita's to raise funds for the new Waco church. Amid colorful crepe paper flowers and tissue paper garlands created by the Chavez family, the Mexican American families enjoyed music and dancing, feasted on tamales and enchiladas, and raised money to build St. Francis church in Waco.[28]

By the end of the twentieth century, only a few Mexican American families still lived in the vicinity of St. Rita's chapel. Used for masses only three times a year—in December, for Our Lady of Guadalupe, in the spring, for Easter, and in June, for St. Rita's Day—the church building fell into disrepair. The bishop of the Austin diocese recognized the importance of the small rural church to the Mexican American families, however, and encouraged St. Francis priests to support its restoration. Built through the devotion of St. Rita's people, St. Francis repaid its debt by sending volunteers to repair the floor, benches, and roof. The addition of fans, new lights, and heaters added to the comfort of the worshippers. St. Francis Knights of Columbus, many of whom descended from the farmers who built St. Rita's, now sell plates of barbecue to raise funds for St. Rita's upkeep.[29]

Rural African American congregations sustained their individual churches through cooperation with other black congregations, without regard for denomination.[30] From their beginnings following emancipation, many African American rural churches met for services only twice a month on alternating weeks. Inability to support the salary of a full-time pastor initially accounted for this practice. Pastors farmed or held other jobs and often served two churches at a time. Rather than decreasing opportunities for social exchange, semimonthly services actually contributed toward broadening the community base for rural church members. Churches in proximity to one another often coordinated their schedules so that families could meet together at one church or another every week. Individual congregations were historically small, with perhaps twenty to fifty active members, limited early on to families within walking distance and later victimized by rural depopulation. Combining forces for worship with other churches multiplied the impact of corporate fellowship. In 1988, when Roosevelt Fields became pastor of Goshen Cumberland Presbyterian Church, in the Harrison community of McLennan County, the congregation met for worship every other Sunday and welcomed regular visitors from neighboring Pilgrim Rest Baptist, which

STAINED GLASS WINDOW, ST. PAUL UNITED CHURCH OF CHRIST, NEAR MARLIN

met on the other Sundays of the month. Likewise, on the Sundays between their own services, most of the Goshen congregation attended services at Pilgrim Rest. Fields said, "Whatever church you went to, you still had the same people because they all fellowshipped together."[31]

In addition to attending regular worship services in neighboring churches, members of rural African American churches shared special events throughout the calendar year. Following a morning in Sunday school or worship in their own church, many faithful African American Christians spent afternoons and nights attending special services in other churches, perhaps a homecoming, a pastor's anniversary service, or revival, or maybe an annual program sponsored by the church mission society, choir, women's organization, or brotherhood. Shared worship styles and mutual social, political, and economic concerns prevailed over denominational differences. Members of the guest churches brought with them not only musical or speaking talents to share, but also financial offerings that provided significant support for the host church. They shared announcements about illnesses and deaths within their individual congregations and prayed together for members away from home in military service.

Mount Pleasant and Mount Olive Missionary Baptist Churches in the Downsville area of southern McLennan County met often with Cedar Grove Baptist Church, located ten miles south near the community of Satin in Falls County. Members of these churches, often related by blood or marriage, considered their three congregations "sister churches" or the "tri-church circle." In addition to taking part in auxiliary, anniversary, and mission services throughout the calendar year, they shared joint services during Holy Week, meeting together from Wednesday through Friday nights preceding Easter, with their three ministers each leading services one night.[32]

Rosena Evans stated that her church, Majors Chapel Methodist, outside Golinda in Falls County, received frequent invitations from other churches "to come to them and render a program for them." Majors Chapel, with about twenty active members, often met with the Mount Zion Baptist Church at Rosenthal or Mount Olive Baptist Church at Downsville. Ushers and musicians from one congregation might assist during special events at another church. The Majors Chapel choir once joined a federation of choirs that traveled between area churches from Satin to Downsville, on either side of the McLennan-Falls County line, sharing the gospel through music.[33]

Springhill Methodist Church, near Riesel, continued for more than 130 years the tradition of sharing monthly community singings and annual homecomings and programs with a core of other longtime congregations: Goshen Cumberland Presbyterian and Pilgrim Rest Baptist Churches in the community of Harrison, and New Zion, Sunset, and Nazareth Baptist Churches just east of the McLennan-Falls County line. The community singings rotated between the churches one Sunday night a month, with each church choir presenting two selections. When a month had five Sundays, the churches shared a missions program on the fifth Sunday. Other churches, including some in Mart, Marlin, or Waco, also cooperated in special services with Springhill.[34]

Barbara Hamilton Williams, speaking of Springhill Methodist, voiced feelings shared by other Christians for their rural churches: "That's where I was born. I'm rooted there. And I love my church, I love my people." Williams attributed the perseverence of her church to "that little faithful few that trusted, had a little trust in God to hang on. And so, if God is willing, we'll be there until the end comes."[35] Indeed, longevity was often the reward for open-country churches where the "faithful few" were related by family past and family present and shared a common ethnic or racial heritage.

CHAPTER 3

Feeling at Home

"NO PLACE IS SO DEAR TO MY CHILDHOOD."

—Little Brown Church in the Vale

*L*IFELONG MEMBERS OF RURAL CHURCHES experienced a flood of memories every time they viewed their church's steeple from a distance, entered the familiar building, sat in a certain pew, or sang a particular hymn. Besides familial and cultural associations, their church evoked a sense of place interwoven with social and personal identity.[1] Speaking of Springhill United Methodist Church, Ernestine Anderson expressed the connection commonly felt by Christians for their rural churches. Anderson claimed that, for her, Springhill church is "like water is to the body, a necessity. I know that I would probably survive without this church," she admitted, "but I don't think I would be complete. I feel at home here, I feel a part of here, and therefore it makes my service to the Lord very comfortable."[2]

Feeling complete, at home, and comfortable grew from connections between the physical landscape and positive, early, social experiences shared by the congregation. Pastor Lawrence G. Felice remarked that members of St. Paul United Church of Christ, six miles north of Marlin in Falls County, "have a real identity in that local area. They can tell you not only who lives in that house now, but who has lived there over the years, and who built it. These are people that when

HATS, GOSHEN CUMBERLAND PRESBYTERIAN CHURCH IN AMERICA, HARRISON

they give you directions, it's names of so-and-so's hill and such-and-such and it's nothing on the map." In 1999, five years beyond its centennial, St. Paul had only seventy-five members, all belonging through birth or marriage to one of three core family groups. When members viewed their church and its surroundings, they perceived much more than the casual passerby, who might count only about fifteen houses between the church and the main highway. Older members remembered

ELDER, GOSHEN CUMBERLAND PRESBYTERIAN CHURCH IN AMERICA, HARRISON

days gone by, between the world wars, when the church and its neighborhood reached their population peak. Just down the hill from the church, at the crossing of two dirt roads, were a school and grocery store, and along the road toward the main highway stood almost a hundred homes, some on small-acreage farms and others as tenant houses on larger farms. The church on the hill boasted a new building, completed in 1920 to replace the original building, damaged in 1914 by lightning. In those days, the congregation enjoyed an orchestra, socialized with all-day picnics, and listened to hour-and-a-half sermons.[3]

Within living memory, churches like St. Paul were the centers for social life for their members. The Baptist congregation at Cego, in Falls County, gathered for ice cream parties, hay rides, potluck dinners-on-the-ground, Valentine and Christmas parties, and oyster suppers. Longtime church members also recalled tacky parties, where everyone dressed up in funny clothing and wigs, and box suppers, where young men bid on dinner boxes packed by young women. Likewise, members of Canaan Baptist Church once enjoyed activities that revolved around the congregation. Summer brought the annual church-wide picnics, when, as Edna Dreyer recalled, "We'd all pack in the car and go to Cameron Park [in Waco] and spend the whole day. We had a big time. Everybody went, from the youngest to the oldest. We carried our lunch and had a picnic lunch. Then, late in the afternoon, someone would go downtown and get some ice cream, and we'd top it off with ice cream." In autumn, the congregation gathered for woodcutting picnics, Dreyer said, when "the men would cut the wood, the women would bring the food, and of course the kids would play." The wood furnished the church with a ready supply for the old stove that was the building's winter heating source. On Christmas Eve the congregation gathered around a candlelit tree to watch children present a program and listen to the pastor's comments on the season. Then, the children received presents and gift bags filled with fruit and candy.[4]

In many instances, the church building and surrounding grounds were the largest places for rural neighbors to congregate for community-wide events. The parish house at St. Paul's Evangelical and Reformed Church, Gerald, served as the center of social life for German Protestant families in northeastern McLennan County between the world wars. Recalling those times, Albert Leuschner remarked, "People had time for the church activities because they were pretty well *the* activities, and so they were primary." The old parish hall, built in 1932 and destroyed in a fire in 1978, had a stage used for Christmas plays, when the children donned costumes and acted out the biblical Christmas story before receiving gifts of candy, apples, and oranges. Also, the Gerald School, located just across the road from the church, used the parish hall stage for its annual plays.[5]

Prior to its 1946 relocation to Satin, Cedar Grove Baptist Church sat within four and a half acres that marked the educational, religious, and social center for African Americans living nearby. In addition to the Baptist church, the land encompassed the only cemetery for miles around, a Methodist church, and the Rock Dam schoolhouse. Lonnie Graves remembered that some classes of the two-room school met in the Baptist church during construction of a third room. As in other southern communities, a special program highlighted the last days of school, and since the Cedar Grove church was the largest meeting place around, it hosted closing-day ceremonies for the school.[6]

For African American communities, nothing outshone annual Juneteenth festivities, held to remember June 19, 1865, the day news of emancipation first reached Texas slaves. Vera Estelle Allen Malone, born in 1902 in the Harrison community, recalled Juneteenth picnics held at Goshen Cumberland Presbyterian Church. The annual event was unique in Malone's memory for two reasons: work ceased on that one day, and treats like soda pop, ice cream, and peanuts were abundant. Glenda Garrett, born forty-nine years after Malone, celebrated Juneteenth at all-day picnics with family and friends at Springhill Methodist Church. Food was an important part of the day's activities, Garrett remembered: "They would get the old bathtubs, number ten tubs, as they called it, packed it down with the soda and the ice cubes. We would have fish fries. We would have barbecue, homemade ice cream." Softball games played by all the members and their children were also a fun part of 1950s Juneteenth picnics at Springhill. Juneteenth celebrations often included a religious service. Churches in the Harrison community sponsored "roving" revivals during the week of June nineteenth. For instance, on one night the Methodist minister preached in the Presbyterian church, the next night the Presbyterian minister preached in the Baptist church, and the third night, the Baptist minister preached in the Methodist church.[7]

In addition to providing worship and educational spaces, the grounds of country churches often held other structures available for community use. Located behind some rural African American churches were unpretentious, unmarked buildings that served as meeting halls for the Prince

HELMETS OF SALVATION, MOUNT PLEASANT MISSIONARY BAPTIST CHURCH, DOWNSVILLE

Hall Masons and their women's auxiliary, the Heroines of Jericho. Wooden tabernacles served Baptist churches at Birome, Cego, Liberty Hill, Osage, and Patton, providing an open-air site for summer services, revival meetings, and social activities. In the late 1920s, Liberty Hill Baptist Church, in southern McLennan County, fashioned a tabernacle from lumber salvaged from the former local schoolhouse, abandoned upon consolidation into Eddy. The Liberty Hill tabernacle had a dirt floor, which a faithful member raked just before services and where mothers laid quilts for sleepy children during services. A wooden platform across the front provided space for choir seats and a piano. This unique tabernacle had wooden sides divided into top-hinged sections, which raised up to allow hilltop breezes to cool worshippers during summer revivals. The tabernacle became the scene of church socials and the site for home demonstration club meetings and fairs.[8]

Familiarity with the rural church, developed over a lifetime, motivated members to active involvement with its physical well-being. The people who worship on Sunday mornings in open-country churches are the same ones who mow the church lawn, dust windowsills, lay out altar cloths, and prepare communion. Inspiration for their devoted service comes from oral tradition passed down through the generations, which stressed the sacrifices of the church founders, who often constructed the first meeting place and furnishings by hand after long days of farm work. Grandparents gathered wood for the stove in winter and arrived at church early to raise the windows in summer. Everyone with a skill, from carpentry to sewing, applied his or her best work to the upkeep and improvement of God's house. At St. Paul's E&R Church, Gerald, members of the Women's Guild spent Saturday afternoons at the church, sweeping, dusting, and mopping in anticipation of the moment the next morning when the sexton walked across the road from his home to ring the bell signaling the arrival of the Lord's Day.[9]

Over time, rural churches, like most farmhouses, became increasingly more comfortable with the advent of new technologies. Canaan Baptist Church, with its recently applied white vinyl siding, shines brightly on the rise at the corner of Canaan Church Road and Coryell City Road west of Crawford. Facilities include the sanctuary, with its single center tower topped with a steeple, an annex with a full kitchen and dining hall, and a classroom and office building connecting the sanctuary and annex. The congregation maintains a residence for its pastor on the next lot west. Central air and heat, cushioned theater-style seating, and an electronic piano accommodate wor-

HELMETS OF SALVATION, MOUNT PLEASANT MISSIONARY BAPTIST CHURCH, DOWNSVILLE

ship in the sanctuary, which is an eastward-facing rectangle, bisected north-south with center wings. The central portion of the building dates to 1894, when the church members constructed a one-room, thirty-foot by fifty-foot wood frame building, with eight hundred dollars' worth of materials and untold hours of donated labor. Along with the sanctuary, the farmers built a parsonage for their first full-time minister. Canaan church families, most of whom initially rented land on shares from founder Heinrich Engelbrecht, raised funds for building materials by each donating their proceeds from one bale of cotton. Engelbrecht, as the landlord, also gave the church his share of the renters' bales. In 1908, a storm blew the sanctuary off its foundation and, after restoring the frame, the farmers braced it with iron rods, which they jokingly called suspenders. Worshippers sat on wood benches and, as was the custom for many years, women and men sat on opposite sides of the room and the children on the front bench. Three kerosene wall lamps, with reflectors, provided dim lighting, a pump organ furnished music, and a wood stove warmed the room in winter. Eventually, hanging Coleman lamps replaced the kerosene ones, radiating a brighter, whiter light from an incandescent mantle. Pulleys brought the lamps down into reach for igniting. The new lamps improved the lighting so much, B. F. Engelbrecht remembered, "We thought, How good can you have it!"

In 1928, Canaan's families opened the sides of the one-room building and added wings north and south. Cleverly designed doors dropped from the ceiling to divide the space into five separate rooms, where Sunday-school classes met. Also added to the former box building were a central tower and steeple. During the same remodeling, the church acquired a Delco battery plant, which provided electricity in the church for lighting and ceiling fans. Housed in a separate structure behind the church, the new device served the congregation until electric power lines reached the area in 1936. At this time, most of the church members also installed Delco battery plants in their homes. Besides better lights, the Delco plants allowed rural families to enjoy refrigerators, remembrance of which inspired B. F. Engelbrecht to exclaim, "We thought, man, we was really living like the city people now!" Subsequent additions and remodeling at Canaan added a baptistery, indoor restrooms, the fellowship annex and connecting educational space, central heating and air-conditioning, and concrete sidewalks and gravel parking areas.[10]

The descendants of faithful founding members continued to maintain rural church buildings and grounds with investments of their own hands-on labor. Memories of personal, up-close involvement at Canaan Baptist Church extend beyond the building to the adjacent cemetery. Before World War II, when a community member died, the Canaan Baptist Church preacher rang the church bell a certain number of times to alert the neighbors. The message dispersed through the area via party line telephones, quickly followed by a call for those with strong backs to serve as gravediggers, a task requiring immediate action. Members of nearby St. John Lutheran Church joined the Baptists in the work. The family of the deceased furnished lunch for the diggers, who faced a formidable task in the rocky soil. B. F. Engelbrecht recalled resorting at times to dynamite to loosen stubborn rocks and reach six feet down. The task, he said, "took all day, all day. Started about nine o'clock in the morning to get it ready for a two o'clock funeral. It's hard work, one pick at a time." Following a brief service in the family home, where the deceased laid in state, the body lovingly washed and prepared for burial by neighbors, the minister led a funeral service at the church and pallbearers carried the casket out the front door to the cemetery. Even before the families left, the weary diggers began replacing the dirt on top of the coffin.[11]

Donated labor and materials helped most rural churches operate debt free, with a legacy of making-do and paying-as-you-go. From their first log church in 1865, members of Springhill Methodist Church advanced to a wood frame building in 1878. That same humble structure still served the congregation sixty-six years later, but in greatly reduced condition. Ernestine Anderson, born in 1937, recalled that in her childhood the cracks between the floorboards were wide enough to allow a child's attention to stray from the sermon toward the work of doodlebugs shaping conical traps in the sand beneath the church. In 1944, Pastor S. A. Keesee began the work of improving the Springhill church by altering the hearts of his congregation, preaching, "God deserves the best there is." That message, Anderson remembered, caused shame among the members over the building's poor condition. The pastor's next step was convincing his congregation that they could have a new building if they worked hard enough to achieve it. His members were second- and third-generation African American tenant farmers and sharecroppers, reconciled to life within a cycle of indebtedness. Experienced in construction, Keesee promised to work alongside his members to tear down the old building and build a new one. The churchmen utilized lumber from the old church and donated their own labor to the construction, while the women prepared food for the builders. While the construction progressed, the congregation met under a brush arbor.

CHURCH MUSEUM, ST. PAUL'S UNITED CHURCH OF CHRIST, GERALD

Remembering their parents' example, Springhill church members made all subsequent improvements and additions without indebtedness. In 1969, they added a fellowship hall, which provided a kitchen and bathroom, a dining hall, which doubled as Sunday-school space, and a small office for the pastor. With the new addition, the congregation covered the exterior walls with asbestos siding and the interior walls with wood paneling. In 1985, Springhill enlarged its sanctuary seating capacity by fifty places and added carpeting and new pews. Then, three years later, a special fundraiser allowed Springhill to brick the exterior of the sanctuary and the adjoining fellowship hall.[12]

When needs arose requiring hired labor and materials, rural church members responded with creativity and imagination to stretch limited cash resources. In the late 1920s, Liberty Hill Baptist Church held a money drive based on a weigh-in. Everyone donated a penny a pound for the amount of their weight toward the purchase of a Delco lighting system for the church. Several rural churches utilized abandoned army buildings after World War II to increase their physical space. With funds provided by the Southern Baptist Home Mission Board, Cego Baptist Church bought a used barrack from Fort Hood army base, moved it to Cego, and adapted it for Sunday-school rooms. St. Joseph's Catholic Church bought an army chapel from Camp Swift at Bastrop, moved it to Elk, and remodeled it for their sanctuary.[13]

Some rural churches relocated over the years but the original sites remained dear to older members. Leo Simmons, born in 1915, and Edna Long, born in 1940, shared strong personal memories of the former site of Goshen Cumberland Presbyterian Church in America, required to move in 1968 by the widening of Texas Highway 6 at Harrison south of Waco. After organizing in 1874, Goshen church met several years under a brush arbor before a wood frame structure was built. Located next to a stock tank, where baptisms took place, the church house sat within a grove of trees that created a shady haven for social events for the Harrison community. Leo Simmons remembered Juneteenth celebrations there, with black and white families sharing baskets of food on long benches built under the trees and playing baseball in the evenings. In addition to dinners-on-the-ground, Edna Long fondly recalled summers in the former church building, when breezes flowing over the water brought cool relief through the open church windows and the steady beat of hand-held fans matched the rhythm of singing voices. Both Simmons and Long associated significant turning points in their youth with the former church building. There a young Leo Simmons observed Elder Moses Wood faithfully and humbly doing "what he had to do" to serve the congregation. Determining then to model Wood's example, Simmons dedicated all his spare time to his church, including sixty-two years' service as elder. Also in the former Goshen church, Edna Long began playing piano for the youth choir when she was just ten years old and had not yet joined the church. Forty-four years later, she was still church pianist.[14]

Social activities brought rural Christians to their churches on special days throughout the year, but Sunday was the day most closely associated with sacred places on the prairies. Like Barbara Williams, born in 1923, the youngest of ten children, rural church members often recalled that attending church on Sunday was not optional. In those days, Williams said, "Your parents didn't ask if you wanted to go to church. You went to church."[15] For churchgoing farm families, Sundays differed remarkably from other days of the week. As spiritual descendants of the Israelites, they sought to honor the fourth commandment, which exhorted, "Remember the Sabbath day, to keep it holy. Six days you shall labor and do all your work, but the seventh day is a Sabbath of the Lord your God; in it you shall not do any work" (Exodus 20: 8-11 New American Standard Bible). Most Christians observed a day of rest on the first day of the week, Sunday, to commemorate Christ's resurrection.

In order to rest from work on Sunday, farm families doubled their Saturday chores. For the Maxwell children, growing up in the South Bosque community in the 1920s, extra work on Saturdays allowed time the next day for attendance at Harris Creek Church, followed by a special Sunday dinner. Geneva Maxwell Russell said, "On Saturday we always cooked a cake or something like that, and if we were going to have chicken, we killed that chicken and dressed it and fixed it ready to cook, and we'd cook it after we'd get home from church. But we always fixed pie or cake or whatever special we were going to have on Saturday. We did as much on Saturday as we could."[16]

When Edwin Massirer married Agnes Gohlke in 1931, he continued his Baptist father's practice of stocking the woodpile on Saturdays to avoid chopping wood on the Sabbath. Although the

MASONIC HALL, SPRINGHILL UNITED METHODIST CHURCH, RIESEL

Massirers milked cows and fed livestock on Sundays, they prepared Sunday's feed the previous day, including husking corn for the chickens. Also on Saturdays Agnes Massirer cooked the main portion of the next day's meals. Saturday's extra work not only allowed time on Sundays to honor God through attending church, it provided rare moments of leisure or recreation. The Massirers enjoyed walking with their dogs along the creeks on their farm on Sunday afternoons.[17]

TABERNACLE, PATTON BAPTIST CHURCH, PATTON

As an adult in the 1930s Albert Huber wanted to honor the tradition of Sunday rest as he had learned in his youth, but he owned a store with gasoline pumps at the crossroads in Cego and his neighbors often came looking for him wanting to buy gasoline. Huber explained that the frugal farmers bought only a gallon or two of gasoline at a time, just enough to cover the immediate round trip, whether to the gin or church or a neighboring farm, so just about every time they used the car they needed to buy gas. Huber fell into the habit of opening the store and gas pumps on Sunday mornings until church services began. Only during cotton-ginning season did he keep the store open all day on Sundays, and then only to accommodate migrant laborers in the area who worked six days a week and spent part of Sunday shopping for the coming week's groceries.[18]

Sundays meant a change of dress and putting on shoes. As long as rural children were at home working or playing, most went barefoot, but school and church meant fitting their feet into shoes and boots. Geneva Russell and her siblings, growing up in South Bosque in the 1920s, had their "Sunday clothes, and that's the only time we wore them, too, is on Sunday. When we got home we took them off, and you know, we didn't wear them around and get them all dirty and nasty." Likewise, Rosalee Smajstrla Urbis and her sister Evelyn Smajstrla Cunningham recalled that Sundays provided the opportunity to wear "your Sunday shoes" and "Sunday dress," set apart for that one day a week from the everyday flour-sack apparel and school shoes. Following World War I, Joe C. Trotter worked in the cotton fields around Falls County during the week and spent Friday night through Sunday morning cleaning and ironing Sunday clothes for other young working men and women. He began his work with a gasoline iron ordered from a catalog but eventually bought an electric iron. Trotter's business improved the appearances of many Baptists and Methodists in the Satin area on Sunday mornings.[19]

For farming families, time off from work on the Sabbath afforded opportunities for socializing with family and friends. Dora Mae Hardcastle Miller, born in 1921, recalled Sundays as being "heaven all through my childhood." Services brimmed with people at Cego Baptist Church before the Great Depression. In the stifling heat of summer, the congregation met in the shade of an open-air tabernacle. Every Sunday following services, the Hardcastle clan gathered at their grandfather's farm for a potluck dinner, prepared by the women the previous day and packed carefully to last

TABERNACLE, GHOLSON CEMETERY, GHOLSON

until Sunday lunchtime. Playing with cousins, surrounded by aunts and uncles, Dora Miller remembered Sunday afternoons as "really wonderful" occasions. A highlight of the day, following the noon meal, was the country and gospel music performed by family members, playing mandolin, guitar, French harp, and fiddles. The family stayed together until time to return to church for the evening service.[20]

The extended families of Canaan Baptist Church likewise gathered to share lunch after Sunday morning services, often inviting the pastor and his family. Meals were simple, according to Minnie Weber Gauer, with homemade bread, butter, and jelly, and sausage from the smokehouse. The men visited together in one room of the house, the women in another, and the children played outside until time for night church services. Ima Hoppe Bekkelund recalled that for farm families at Canaan Baptist Church fellowship continued on after the night services. She said that even though the cows at home still had to be milked, "when we got out of church we didn't just run off and go straight home like we do now. We all mingled around and talked, and the kids played and everything else out there."[21]

For the Hanak family, who immigrated to McLennan County in 1907 from Czechoslovakia, afternoons following Sunday services at St. Martin's Church, Tours, were "visiting days," with families alternating as hosts. The women prepared generous meals for a crowd, which might number forty-five or more, and cleaned up afterwards, sharing news and gossip as they worked. The men relaxed, drinking coffee or beer, and talked. As Mary Hanak Simcik remembered more than sixty years later, the children would "run around like crazy, climb trees and everything else."[22]

Among the Norwegian Lutherans in Bosque County, Sunday night brought singings in the homes of church members, who alternated serving as hosts. Oris Pierson recalled that making music together was the sole purpose of the meetings; the singers expected no refreshments. Although morning worship services were solemn occasions, in the evening singings, the Piersons and their Lutheran friends "just sang our hearts out!" Gospel hymns, some borrowed from the Methodists and Baptists, dominated the singings. Around July the Fourth, patriotic songs were popular. Pierson, a choir member for more than fifty-five years, credited the early-twentieth-century Sunday singings for a strong music tradition displayed by Bosque County Lutheran churches in the 1970s.[23]

Appreciation for the service of ancestors in building and maintaining a church facility and shared memories of social opportunities and Sunday rituals there engendered loyalty and affection. Recognition of individual growth and development experienced in that certain place produced a layer of identity close to one's heart. Before World War II, especially among women and African

Americans, the church provided a place to try on leadership roles unavailable to them in the general society.

In a time when southern society limited an African American's self-improvement, the church was an important place for rural people to develop natural talents. In the 1940s, Reverend S. A. Keesee of Springhill Methodist Church told his congregation they needed to cultivate their young people for God's service so that the church would persist when he and his generation were gone. The only young people in the church then were about a dozen girls and young women, whose fathers were mostly sharecroppers and whose mothers worked as domestics in Waco, commuting more than thirty miles daily. Algie Keesee, the pastor's wife, volunteered to donate her time to teach piano lessons in her home to four of the girls. The girls did not have pianos at home on which to practice, but used keyboards printed on cardboard. More than fifty years later, Ernestine Anderson remembered Sister Keesee's strict discipline during lessons: "When we hit a wrong note she'd hit us on our knuckles with a wooden ruler. And when I went home to tell Mother about it, she said, 'Well, maybe you shouldn't hit a wrong note.'"

In the Springhill tradition, the accompanist conducted the choir from the piano, so Pastor Keesee encouraged his wife's pupils to gain experience by playing for the church choirs. When the young pianists lost their places on a song and fell behind, Keesee urged, "Sing on, Choir," and they eventually learned to keep pace. Once when Ernestine Anderson lost her place in the music, she began to cry. Pastor Keesee stopped the service and reminded her, "When you do the best you can, there's no reason to cry." His patient encouragement helped all four of Algie Keesee's students to continue their practice until they became choir leaders in adulthood. After fifty years, two of them continued leading the Springhill music service on alternating Sundays. On second Sundays of each month, one played the piano and led the Senior Choir, while the other played the organ. On fourth Sundays, they traded instruments and the pianist led the New Faith Choir.[24]

Lonnie Graves was an African American farmer in Falls County who loved music, and Cedar Grove Baptist Church gave him a place to express his passion. In the last two decades of the twentieth century the Cedar Grove choir gained widespread recognition for excellence. A large part of their success was attributable to raw talent, which showed itself in the years before World War II, when Graves's mother brought back to the youth choir songs she heard sung at the annual

FESTIVAL, ST. RITA'S CATHOLIC CHURCH, SATIN

FESTIVAL, ST. RITA'S CATHOLIC CHURCH, SATIN

FESTIVAL, ST. RITA'S CATHOLIC CHURCH, SATIN

Baptist association meetings. Without benefit of sheet music, she just sang hymns for the choir that were new to them, like "The Church in the Wildwood" and "Sunshine in My Soul," and the choir quickly picked up the tune, words, and harmony. When members of the youth choir grew old enough to attend associational meetings, Graves reported, "We could go to the association and hear a choir sing a song one time and come back home and sing that song! Have the words! Have the tune! Have the music and everything and remember it. I don't know how we did it. But this is actually a fact. We heard the song one time and together we kids would all just remember the words. We would put it together."

Cedar Grove Baptist Church, however, experienced a frequent turnover in pianists. In the 1940s, when Lonnie Graves was a young husband with a growing family, he became president of the church choir and took up the challenge of finding a pianist. He remembered arriving at a solution that changed his life and answered the church's need. "So finally it just got so acute till sometimes we'd have somebody to play and sometimes we wouldn't. And I went to the church one day and I said, 'Lord, I would just like to learn how to play the piano well enough to where I could help the church out, where I could play.'" Graves spent evenings after work at church, picking out tunes on the piano "as best I could with this prayer in my heart, that I could be serviceable to the church where I wouldn't have to be worrying ourselves so much about this." Eventually Graves bought an old used piano from the Satin Methodist Church and continued to practice at home, still picking out songs by ear. Later, when he took his daughter to Waco for piano lessons, he stayed and listened and learned all he could. Additional training came from a fellow farm laborer, a young Mexican man who played guitar and violin and taught Graves some basic music theory. "So with all of these things," he recalled, "I just kind of put them together, and my knowledge. And I would just sit down and look at the song and slowly pick the song out."[25]

In the Jim Crow South, churches fostered the only place for full freedom of expression for African Americans. Before and during the Civil Rights movement, African Americans in rural Central Texas were cautious. Through prayer they supported the boycotts, sit-ins, and marches televised on the evening news, but took no overt action that endangered their livelihoods or families. The elders preached prudence, with past oppressions still clear in their minds. They went only to the back doors of Anglo homes where they worked or made deliveries, on Saturdays in

FATHER FERNANDO HERNANDEZ IN DOORWAY, ST. RITA'S CATHOLIC CHURCH, SATIN

Waco they did not sit at dining counters in places that did not want them, and they stayed within the few blocks of the town square where black-owned or immigrant-run stores, cafes, and theaters welcomed them. As a child during the 1940s, Ernestine Anderson overheard her parents and other adult members of Springhill Methodist Church talking among themselves of the need to be careful. "I gathered then from what they would say," she recalled, "blacks at dusk needed to be at home or within the confines of their community. You did not go to Riesel at night. I never heard them actually say that it was the Klan, but there were those groups that if you were in the wrong place at the wrong time, you may not be heard of or seen again, or if found, you'd be beaten." In those days recourse for African American victims of violence and crime was limited. "I remember the elderly named certain constables, I think they were called then," Anderson said, "and that this was a good constable; if you needed him you could call on him, but you better be careful who you accuse. So you could call on him to keep the peace or whatever, but if you accuse Mister over here, it wasn't going to mean anything. They were going to say you were lying or whatever, so you just wouldn't get anywhere." Taught early in life that security lay in obeying the rules of segregation, Anderson believed, "The safest two places I knew was my church and my home."[26] Originally located within walking distance of members' homes, in neighborhoods strictly segregated by race, within the physical and spiritual family circle, rural black churches provided safe places for African Americans to gather, to organize, to serve their communities, and to instruct their children, without fear, even at night.[27]

Church auxiliary organizations provided significant leadership opportunities for African American men and women in a period when the outside world prevented their educational, social, and economic advancement. Women, especially, took advantage of the opportunity to take charge for at least a few hours a week. Cedar Grove Baptist Church credited its founding and improvement largely to women. Five women—Matilda London, Sookie Buryer, Salina King, Emma Graves, and Emma Masters—assembled with two men, Bonnie Buryer and Ned Smith, to establish the church soon after learning of their emancipation. In 1898, the churchwomen, led by Emma Masters, organized a Women's Missionary Society. Not until 1940 did the churchmen organize a parallel Brotherhood society. The women of the church received credit, too, for organizing the junior department and junior mission group.[28] African American women, the same as their white counterparts, first applied their talents and skills to work among women and children in Sunday school and mission organizations. Auxiliaries like Woman's Missionary Society provided women a break from the routine of farm work and housekeeping. Through mission societies, women raised funds for building repairs and upkeep and for benevolent causes within the congregation and beyond.[29]

In some cases, African American women had more freedom than white women to assume roles before the full church. Laywomen led the choir, voiced corporate prayers, and opened the church service by singing a slow gospel hymn. Barbara Williams, a member of Springhill United Methodist Church since her christening in 1923 and longtime leader in the choir and women's missions society, received training as a Methodist lay leader so that she could conduct worship services in the absence of the pastor. During the 1970s, her son-in-law was Springhill's pastor, and Williams substituted for him on Sundays when he was away. Almost thirty years later, her current minister remarked that Williams's influence on the congregation remained "vital" to her own work as pastor. With an active membership that was primarily female and over the age of fifty, Springhill church depended heavily on women like Williams and her friend Pauline Miller, who founded the church's cemetery association and coordinated it for more than thirty-five years, and also served as church treasurer and head usher.[30]

African American women also served Central Texas rural churches as full-time pastors and as co-pastors with their husbands. Early in life Carol Grant Gibson felt that God called her for special service, but being Baptist and a woman, she did not think her ministry would be pastoral. Then, when she met and married a Methodist pastor, she thought, "This is what God would have me do, work through someone else." Nevertheless, Gibson continued to sense "a real urging from God to do something more." In 1990, she entered the ministry and two years later received her first appointment as pastor with the United Methodist Church. In 1996, after serving congregations in Wichita and Williamson Counties, Gibson received the joint charge of two historic United Methodist churches in McLennan County: Bracks Chapel, established in Waco in 1876, and Springhill, originated by freedpeople in the Brazos River bottoms in 1865.[31]

Anglo, Czech, and German women also found the church needful of and receptive to their services. Catholic women working through the Altar Society served rural congregations like St. Joseph's at Elk by providing service and attention to parishioners when sickness struck, decorating

VIRGEN DE GUADALUPE, ST. RITA'S CATHOLIC CHURCH, SATIN

the altar with flowers, and assisting with the annual picnic and auction fundraiser. For many years, St. Joseph's raised its annual operating funds during one weekend in July by sponsoring bingo games and selling fried chicken dinners. All the cooking took place across the road from the church in the Smajstrla home, where the church women filled the kitchen, frying chicken and boiling potatoes in wash pots on a hot wood stove, while young men ran the food across the road to the church for sale.[32]

Going about their work without drawing much attention, women in German Evangelical and Reformed churches taught children's Sunday-school classes, played the pump organ for church services, sang in the choir, prepared meals for grieving families after funerals, furnished covered dish dinners for happier occasions, conducted vacation Bible schools, and met together for the Women's Guild or Ladies Aid Society. They sent cookies to young men from the congregation serving in World War II. Eventually, as the membership of the churches shrank, women assumed additional leadership roles, including church council service. Although greatly diminished in number, the Women's Guild of St. Paul's United Church of Christ, Cego, still met at the turn of the twenty-first century. The women's group there outlived the Sunday-school program. They met once monthly, on Wednesday evenings in the summer months and following a Sunday worship service during the winter months. As their mothers before them, the women gathered supplies for missionaries on foreign fields. They packed kits of toiletries for Church World Service to help people caught in natural disasters, such as hurricanes in Central America, and they sewed bibs and lap robes for nursing home residents. An active participant in the Women's Guild of St. Paul's United Church of Christ, Gerald, Janet Terry Silaff donated oil paintings and handicrafts for its annual bazaar. "I feel like the things that I do are meaningful maybe to someone else, and especially to the younger people," she explained, adding, "I'm not one to get up and make speeches or anything like that, but I try to live the life that I've always grown up to live, and I'm hoping that eventually this will shine down there at St. Paul's. Someone will see it and realize that our church did mean something to us."[33]

From the 1930s German American women met once or twice a month at Canaan Baptist Church for missions activities. Sometimes they brought their children, but often the fathers watched the children at home for the rare hour when their wives were away. The women spent the hour

COUNTRY WEDDING, ST. PAUL UNITED CHURCH OF CHRIST, NEAR MARLIN

FLOWER GIRL, COUNTRY WEDDING, ST. PAUL UNITED CHURCH OF CHRIST, NEAR MARLIN

studying North American Baptist Conference mission work around the world and doing projects, especially sewing baby layettes or rolling bandages for mission hospitals, a denominational effort called White Cross. The women also collected medicine bottles and old eyeglasses for the mission fields. They raised funds for special church furnishings, such as offering plates, communion linens, and a silver tea service. By the 1970s, many women in the congregation worked outside the home, so Canaan's women changed their meeting times from weekdays to Sundays, meeting an hour before evening worship services. By 1999, White Cross work became a family-oriented project, with children and men participating with the women in rolling bandages for foreign mission hospitals.[34]

Rural churches, led by the women, participated as well as they could in providing donations for worldwide missions, but many felt like the member of Liberty Hill Baptist Church who reported, "As far as missions goes, we always feel that mission starts at home. If one of our families are in need, they get the money or they get the bread or whatever it is that they need at the time." Churches responded to needs among their rural neighbors in cases of hardship, helping furnish groceries or clothing for families struggling to make ends meet. Families with many children often received garden produce and canned goods from churchwomen's groups who knew of their need. Older members of rural churches recalled the days when men and women sat up through the night with sick neighbors and helped bring in a family's crop when the father fell ill.[35]

Memories, some real and some imagined, evoke awareness of connection between people and places. For lifelong members of persistent open-country churches, sensory perceptions of the physical, constructed church elicited feelings of identification and belonging with historical, social, and spiritual foundations. As one pastor explained, "That's where they were baptized, confirmed, married, buried friends" and that's "where they find God's love. That's what keeps them coming."[36]

CHAPTER 4

Serving the Lord

"HOW PRECIOUS DID THAT GRACE APPEAR,
THE HOUR I FIRST BELIEVED."

—*Amazing Grace*

IN THE CENTRAL TEXAS RURAL CHURCH, horizontal interpersonal relationships intersect the vertical relationship between the individual and God. Longtime members began there as infants, progressed through the Sunday school from preschool to adulthood, and attended worship services, revivals, and holy day events. A lifetime of spiritual development led Glenda Garrett to confess, "I consider myself a child of God. I can say I try to live a Christian life. I slip and slide along the way as everyone does, but I feel that Springhill [Methodist Church] is my home not only because my family was there, I have my soul there at Springhill."[1]

Reflecting their separate denominational doctrines, rural Texas churches espoused various methods for entrance into church membership. In Baptist churches, the first step toward belonging occurred when an individual repented of sin and accepted salvation through Jesus Christ. At the end of a fervent sermon, usually during an annual revival meeting, the evangelist appealed to those making such decisions, called professions of faith, to come forward to the altar and give witness to a

CHURCH DOOR, PATTON
BAPTIST CHURCH, PATTON

changed life. Thus reborn into the Christian life, the individual could request full membership in the church. Often, the church would double-check the sincerity of the conversion and would put the matter to a vote before the congregation. Those who committed their lives to Christ then received baptism by immersion in creeks or farm tanks. Catholic, Lutheran, and German Evangelical and Reformed congregations baptized infants by aspersion (sprinkling) or affusion (pouring). Upon reaching early adolescence, young people attended a series of catechism classes to learn church doctrine. At the end of the classes, they exhibited their new knowledge before the congregation and became fully confirmed members. In rural African American Methodist churches, infants were sprinkled, but when they attained school age, children became accountable for experiencing a personal spiritual encounter to which they could testify before their elders. Having proven their salvation through their story, young people were baptized again, with the choice of being immersed or sprinkled. The Sunday school prepared children's hearts to receive salvation and taught new church members to become worthy disciples. The rural pastor or priest played a vital role in all these religious experiences and was the one to whom the church turned for spiritual guidance through all of life's major events.

In cotton's heyday, rural Baptists timed their annual revival meetings to harvest souls during the lull between planting and picking. In the South Bosque area, west of Waco, people came from miles around to services held in the shade of a brush arbor at Harris Creek Church. Mothers brought quilts and made pallets for sleepy youngsters and nursed hungry infants during the long evenings. In later years, the community held revivals beneath a large live oak tree. County road crews furnished lumber from bridge timbers for construction of a platform under the tree to hold the choir benches, pulpit, and piano, and the crowd sat in folding chairs on the ground. Visiting preachers stayed in church members' homes during revival week and the hosts prepared their meals.

The measure of a revival's success at Harris Creek was not only in the number of converts made, but also the extent to which the preacher inspired Granny Barton to shout. By the 1930s, Melissa Waldrip Barton, born in antebellum Georgia and an ardent Confederate, was one of the oldest women in the South Bosque community, and her sweet disposition, small stature, and reputation for good cooking earned her the affectionate title of Granny among the entire community. "My grandmother was one of these shouting kind," recalled her descendant, Geneva Maxwell Russell. Granny Barton's shouting sometimes surprised unwary revival preachers. Family tradition held that one time Granny Barton commenced shouting when her grandson walked to the altar to rededicate his life, and the visiting preacher asked the school principal, standing nearby, how he should respond. The principal, who knew Granny's fervor well, answered, "Nothing, just let her go." Sometimes, the congregation accused revival preachers of lengthening their sermons and raising the emotional pitch just to solicit a shout from Granny Barton. Mary Ellen Nix Bullock, who attended Harris Creek revivals as a child in the 1930s, described Granny's shout as a special yell that continued until she was completely hoarse. "She was just praising the Lord with everything she had, and she was just a tiny, tiny little lady," Bullock remembered.

The Harris Creek 1921 summer revival was especially memorable. The Volunteer Band, a group of students from Baylor University, traveled to South Bosque to assist the pastor with the revival. Geneva Russell's uncle, Warren Barton, a member of the Volunteer Band, transported students to and from Waco in his car. Early in the week response to the revival meetings was slow, and Russell said, "the people just were not moved for some reason during this revival." About midweek, Warren Barton left South Bosque for Baylor to pick up students for the evening services. Unfortunately, he reached the railroad crossing at the center of the community at the same time as the daily train. He was killed instantly by the impact. As news spread of the accidental death of the popular young man, response to the revival meeting reversed from lukewarm to passionate. Russell recalled that for the rest of the week all the people who attended responded to an altar call, becoming converted or rededicating their lives. "It just seemed that it took that, which was sad, and it was very sad to me at the time, just a child, but you could just see a difference in the revival, and just many, many lives were saved after that."[2]

Up until the late 1950s, Cego Baptist Church held revivals in an outdoor tabernacle, an open-sided structure made of materials more permanent than a brush arbor. In midsummer, when the crops were laid by, farm families gathered beneath the tabernacle to hear a guest evangelist preach. Services met mornings and evenings, beginning always on the Friday night before the third Sunday in July and extending ten days to a culminating service on the fourth Sunday. In preparation for

INTERIOR, PATTON BAPTIST CHURCH, PATTON

revival, the choir moved the piano out of the sanctuary to a platform in the tabernacle and faithful members gathered for prayer meetings. The sermons, Edith McKee recalled, carried messages laced with "hellfire and brimstone." Lorene Wittner remembered one revival preacher who broke into his message occasionally to shout, "Are you listenin'?" The people "would sit up," recalled Wittner, because "he'd just scare us to death." Toward the last day, in order to pay the visiting preacher something for his ministry, the church treasurer staged an auction, asking, Who'll give ten dollars? Who'll give five dollars? He worked his way down to one dollar, and people gave what they could. The hundred dollars or so raised at the auction, plus his room and board in church members' homes, compensated the evangelist for his ten days' work.[3]

The Cego revivals were remarkable for the number of Christian conversions inspired during the services. One witness recalled an evening when the line of people responding to the invitation time following the sermon stretched "across the front all the way the full length and out to the road." Dora Miller made her profession of faith at a Cego revival the summer she was twelve years old. She

NEW HOPE BAPTIST CHURCH, RIESEL

recalled her feelings when the evangelist gave the invitation to follow Christ: "I just couldn't stand still and it just seemed like something was taking me up there. I said that was a feeling that I will never forget. I think when about anybody is truly saved that they do know." Lorene Wittner was eleven years old when a neighbor invited her to the 1920 Cego revival. Her parents did not attend church anywhere at that time, so when Wittner made her profession of faith at the revival, she went home and told her parents she wanted to become a Baptist. Her parents insisted, however, that she be sprinkled and become a member of the Methodist church. Ten years later, to please her mother, Lorene remained a Methodist after her marriage to a Baptist. Years later, when Wittner's son was nine years old and someone asked him if he was going to be a Methodist or a Baptist, he replied, "I'm not going to be anything." That confession prompted Lorene Wittner to join her husband's church and be baptized by immersion the same day. Three months later her son joined the church. "I wanted to be a Baptist all along," claimed Wittner, adding, "I'm different than the average Baptist. I'm a Baptist by choice."[4]

Canaan Baptist Church reserved opportunities for professions of faith and baptisms until annual revival season. Lutheran neighbors attended Canaan's revival services, held in the German language until the 1930s. English-speaking families in the area also visited the revival meetings. One witness claimed that the outsiders "experienced the spirit of the meeting" in spite of the language differences. The 1925 revival at Canaan Baptist Church lasted two weeks and included morning and evening services. More than fifty years later, both Edna Dreyer and Marvin Engelbrecht remembered a talk presented by a woman to the young people in one of the revival's morning services. The presentation was significant because it was in English, not German, and because the speaker illustrated her lesson by drawing scenes on a chalkboard. As Engelbrecht recalled, she drew a long river that began narrow and grew wider and wider. Along the river's course she drew lines that represented ten years of a person's life. She pointed out that as the years passed in life and the river became wider, it became harder and harder to cross over to acceptance of Christ. The lesson struck home and a crowd of young people, including Dreyer and Engelbrecht, made their professions of faith that morning.

In those days, Canaan's deacons visited those who made such decisions, praying with them, answering questions, and testing the sincerity of each new convert before accepting them into full membership. In 1925, along with Edna Dreyer and Marvin Engelbrecht, twenty-two other candi-

EXTERIOR, CEGO BAPTIST CHURCH, CEGO

INTERIOR, CEGO BAPTIST CHURCH, CEGO

dates looked forward to their baptisms. That summer, however, drought dried up the creek that served as the church's baptistery. After rain returned in September, the church set the first Sunday in November for its baptism, but that day, Engelbrecht remembered, "come a little old norther and a little rain, and that stopped that." The baptism was postponed almost a year, until September 1926, when Rev. C. C. Laborn immersed a host of children and adults in Rainey Creek.[5]

Baptism services following annual revivals were significant events for the entire community. Carl Neal, who attended Harris Creek Church from his birth in 1921 to his death in 1995, recalled that baptisms were "quite a to-do and a community turnout." He said everyone came. "It didn't make a difference, they may not have been at church all year, but they'd go to the baptizing." The scene described by Roosevelt Fields, when he received baptism in 1963 following his profession of faith in Mount Olive Baptist Church, could have occurred a half-century earlier. The church gathered on the banks of the Brazos River to witness the immersion of about twelve new converts. The women sang "Let us go down to Jordan," while the deacons and minister stood in the water to welcome the candidates. "It's an experience that you'll never forget," claimed Fields.[6]

Memories of conversion experiences in African American Baptist and Methodist churches up into the 1960s included time spent by children and young people on the mourner's bench. During revivals, churches reserved the front bench for school-aged youth who had not made professions of faith in Christ. The yearly evangelistic meetings, followed by annual baptisms, provided a focused effort for the church to reach its young people. Parents, grandparents, aunts, uncles, Sunday-school teachers, and choir members all joined the presiding minister in praying for the salvation of the youngsters on the mourner's bench. Following the sermon, the pastor invited those who felt ready to come before the church with their testimony of salvation.

Roosevelt Fields, born in 1951, grew up, he recalled, "under the old-timey religion" at Mount Olive Missionary Baptist Church, where children began sitting on the mourner's bench at age six or seven. With few exceptions, most children made professions of faith when they were about ten or twelve. When children came forward to confess salvation, church elders examined them closely. "If you got up and you didn't have a testimony, something about those old folks back during that time, they would tell you, say, You really don't have it," Fields said. The elders told the youngsters, "You've got to go back, and once the Lord begin to start to speaking to you, you'll know, you'll have something to say." Although the "old folks" in Fields's home church had little formal education, he explained, "They knew the Lord, and because they knew the Lord it was very important that we as children knew the Lord." The examination process provided assurance that a child was truly saved, with evidence of the indwelling of the Holy Spirit, so that the child would grow into an adult who was steadfast in the faith. Joining the church without "that real true religion, really

FAMILY, SPRINGHILL UNITED METHODIST CHURCH, RIESEL

knowing God," Fields explained, might cause a person to drop out of church later in life, "when things begin to start getting rough." Fields said, "If you truly been born of the spirit of God, when the storm gets so rough in your life, you know who you can lean on."[7]

Members at Springhill United Methodist Church also recalled experiences on the mourner's bench. In the mid-1930s, when she was about twelve years old, Barbara Williams made a profession of faith from the mourner's bench. In the 1940s, Ernestine Anderson knew at invitation time that all eyes in the church were upon her. She said, "I used to get the feeling that the evangelist felt like his revival was a success or failure by the people that came to join the church." Anderson confessed, "For some reason I just never could be ready for revival. I ended up on more mourner's benches probably than anybody in the whole Springhill church." One obstacle in Anderson's way was the thought of baptism by immersion. Having her head "dunked" by the pastor in a farm tank frightened her and she feared drowning. Anderson remembered her mother's encouraging words, "Baby, when you have the spirit in you, you don't think about that," but the girl thought to herself, "Whether I have the spirit or not, I think about living!" When she finally joined the church, relief replaced fear when her Methodist minister gave her a choice between immersion and sprinkling. Of course, Anderson chose sprinkling, and she reported fifty years later, "I feel okay with it because I have never changed my mind on water!"

In the 1960s, Anderson's younger sister, Glenda Garrett, reached the age to sit on the mourner's bench. She recalled young people sitting on the front bench every week, not just at revival time. "I can remember sitting on the front pew a lot of Sundays, and you didn't giggle, you didn't talk, you didn't chew gum, you didn't eat candy and pacify them with cookies like they do in church now," Garrett said. When a child sat on the front row, she faced the choir, and "all the old sisters sitting up there, they're looking right at you." Also, Garrett recalled, sitting behind the children were "the older ones," who disciplined the front row with "a whole lot of knuckles in the back of our head if we did do wrong [and] a little pulling of the ear." Attention to behavior allowed the children to concentrate on listening. "When you went to church and you sat on that front row, you was there to learn," Garrett said. Furthermore, parents tested their children after services. According to Garrett, "When you got home, Mom and Dad was going to ask you, What was church about? What did the preacher talk about today? What did you get out of it?" Glenda Garrett left her seat on the mourner's bench

when she was twelve or thirteen years old and made her profession of faith. Unlike her sister, Garrett chose immersion and was baptized in a farm tank up the road from the church.[8]

In congregations that began as German Evangelical and Reformed churches and later became part of the United Church of Christ, infants received baptism and young people took confirmation classes to become full church members. Lawrence G. Felice, pastor at St. Paul United Church of Christ, north of Marlin, confessed that the emphasis on spiritual rebirth presented in the national media in the last half of the twentieth century raised frequent discussions among the lifelong members of his church. He reported, "Most of the members of St. Paul church cannot remember a time when they didn't believe in God, and therefore they don't have a particular event that was a watershed experience or an epiphany."[9]

GRAVE MARKER, MOUNT OLIVE CEMETERY, DOWNSVILLE

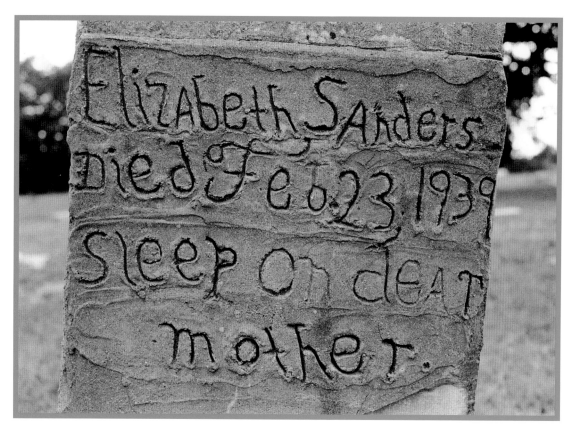

GRAVE MARKER, GOSHEN CEMETERY, HARRISON

Through the twentieth century, changes in confirmation classes among rural German Evangelical and Reformed congregations paralleled changes in the society at large. Hattie Lehmann Leuschner, born in 1909, completed confirmation in 1923 at St. Paul's Church, Gerald. The Lehmann farm was several miles from the church, and she and her older sister drove a buggy on rough roads to confirmation classes, taking their lunches with them for the long ride. The classes, led by Pastor J. Link, were in German, just as church services were then, and the Lehmann family spoke German at home. A few years later, as English became more common, the confirmands stood in front of the congregation and answered questions in German and then repeated them in English. In later life, one lamented, "I got the Apostle's Creed question twice, and I had to do it in English and German, and the other people in the class got the easy questions, like John 3:16."

Hattie Leuschner's cousin, Herman Blankenstein, born in 1916, and his sister, one year younger, took confirmation classes at St. Paul's, Gerald, in 1930. At home, during their preschool years, the Blankenstein children spoke mostly German, mixed with a little English, but when they reached school age, their mother, Annie Carrie Kreder Blankenstein, declared to her husband, parents, and parents-in-law, "Now, look, this broken English has to quit. We're going to speak English. We're here in America and that's what's going to be." Gradually, Herman and his sister forgot much of the German language learned in their earlier years. When they reached thirteen and fourteen years of age and became eligible for confirmation classes at St. Paul's Church, they anticipated having to memorize their lessons in German, as their Uncle Albert Kreder, just a few years their senior, had done. That year, however, to their relief, the church changed the confirmation class and examination from German to English.

In 1932, the summer Irene Otto Blankenstein turned fourteen and entered confirmation classes at St. Paul's, Gerald, about a dozen young people gathered at the church four afternoons a week to study with their pastor. In the early mornings, just after sunrise, Irene Blankenstein went out to the front porch of her parents' farmhouse and studied her lesson for the day. Later, after completing morning chores, she walked a long, hot, three miles to church. The six weeks of classes culminated in an evening service where the young people sat in front of the congregation, reciting one by one their assigned memory verse and answering one question each from the pastor.

By 1950, Albert Leuschner remembered, older people at St. Paul's, Gerald, told his confirmation class that "we were lucky we didn't have to memorize near as much as they used to have to." Confirmation classes for Leuschner were "both great fun and educational." Memorization still took place, but, with less material to cover, there was time to play Ping-Pong in the parish hall and other games outdoors. In the early 1950s, Pastor John Mueller recognized among St. Paul's married adults a number of cases wherein only one of the pair was a full member of the church. For instance, Janet Terry Silaff grew up in Baptist and Church of Christ congregations and married

William Frederick Silaff, who was confirmed at St. Paul's in his adolescence. Pastor Mueller offered confirmation classes to the spouses who were not full members and required attendance from the member spouses as well. About eight couples attended the adult confirmation classes, and William Silaff remarked to his wife, "I got more out of your confirmation than I got out of mine."

At the end of the twentieth century, the number of potential confirmands at St. Paul's, Gerald, was greatly reduced and widely scattered. Eligible teenagers from ninth through eleventh grades lived over a broad area, from Lorena in southwestern McLennan County to Abbott, across the northeastern McLennan County line in Hill County. They all kept busy in multiple after-school organizations. Jane Lovett, who pastored the joint West-Gerald charge from 1997 to 1999, faced the task of arranging confirmation classes for them. "To find a time and a place where we can pull those young people that are all active in their school activities together is going to be quite a challenge," Lovett stated.[10]

From 1922 to 1942, while St. Joseph's Catholic Church was a mission of Assumption Parish in Waco, Sisters of Charity from Providence Hospital held confirmation classes in Elk. Walter Dulock, Rosalee Smajstrla Urbis, and Evelyn Mae Smajstrla Cunningham attended religious classes every Wednesday after school from the time they started first grade to the time they were confirmed at about twelve years old. They studied the Baltimore Catechism by rote and memorized prayers but also had some fun. They played baseball with the nuns and fondly remembered Sister Bernice, who left a lasting impression for running bases in "that old blue heavy garb" with her upturned wimple bouncing up and down like "old wings."

Thoroughly prepared and acculturated into the church, the young people attended an area-wide annual confirmation service under the leadership of the bishop of the Diocese of Galveston, which then included Waco and environs. When time came for Rosalee Smajstrla Urbis and her friends in Elk to receive confirmation, a heavy thunderstorm flooded Tehuacana Creek, and the only vehicle capable of carrying the girls safely across was her father's truck. The children rode in the back end of the truck, standing up all the way and "hoping it wouldn't rain because we'd have really been like wet mice." They reached St. Mary's convent in Waco, where the girls quickly changed into their new white dresses before heading for the church. The rain delayed the bishop's arrival and postponed the confirmation, so John Smajstrla carried the girls to the home of an acquaintance, where they changed back into their everyday clothes and went barefoot rather than soil their good shoes. When word came of the bishop's successful arrival, a scramble to clean up, dress, and don shoes ensued, but, as Urbis recalled, "we got there and sure enough, the bishop came, and so we were confirmed."

During the 1930s two young people from St. Joseph's studied beyond confirmation in order to become altar boys. By attending special classes, Walter Dulock and Billy Yowell learned to assist the celebration of the Eucharist, through lighting candles, responding in Latin to the priest's prayers, carrying the wine and water to the priest, chiming the bell, and holding the paten during communion. They wore black cassocks with white surplices. Walter Dulock began service as altar boy in the Catholic church in Waco when he was a youngster of seven or eight and completed his service at Elk at the age of twenty-eight.[11]

❧ ❧

Revival conversions and confirmation classes supplemented religious lessons learned by rural youth in Sunday school. Between the world wars, when farming was still a viable livelihood on the Blackland Prairie, third- and fourth-generation German Americans filled Evangelical and Reformed churches in Gerald, Cego, Otto, and St. Paul on Sunday mornings. Albert Leuschner recalled that in those days Sunday classes at St. Paul's, Gerald, overflowed from the parish house into the sanctuary and filled the small altar and bell tower rooms. Wilma Altus Richter enjoyed the brightly colored Bible story pamphlets and proudly gave one penny each week for the Sunday-school offering. Teachers were often related to their pupils, and Donald Richter's mother and father taught his classes throughout his youth. Youngsters received "tickets" in Sunday school, which were small memory cards with a colorful illustration of a Bible character or story and a scripture verse to memorize each week.[12]

St. Paul's, Cego, also reached its peak attendance in the 1930s, and minutes of the Sunday-school board indicated the energy engendered by the crowds. In 1938, for instance, the board ordered a total of seventy-two books for its six classes, in English for children and young people and in German for the adult class. Women taught the children's classes, men, the young people's groups, and the pastor taught the adult class. In those days, all the members of the Sunday-school

GRAVE MARKER,
WILLOW GROVE
CEMETERY, WILLOW
GROVE

board were men, but all the members of the only adult Sunday-school class were women. During the Sunday-school period, adult men reportedly congregated outside on the church grounds, visiting with one another until church services began.[13]

Sunday-school teachers wielded strong influence on their youthful charges in rural churches. For Helen Miller, memories of Sunday school at St. Paul's, Cego, during the 1950s rested not upon lessons studied or Bible verses learned, but upon one special teacher, Anita Zimmerman. Although Zimmerman was one of the few adults in the church to whom St. Paul's many Miller children were not kin, they called her Aunt Anita anyway. "She was just one of those really loving people that all the kids always liked, and she was perfect for her Sunday-school teaching job," recalled Miller.[14]

Several members of Springhill Methodist Church recalled classes led by Hannah Hamilton in the 1940s. Ernestine Anderson remembered that Sunday school lasted an hour, and Hamilton spent about twenty minutes of that time teaching the weekly Bible lesson and memory verse, printed on colorful cards. Then she questioned her pupils on the lesson, because at the beginning of the church service, the adults quizzed them again on what they had learned. Anderson's favorite part of Sunday school was a period of about fifteen minutes when her teacher just talked with the youngsters, providing counsel and guidance. Before the end of the Sunday-school hour, Hamilton shared light refreshments with her pupils, usually home-baked cupcakes or other treats. Outside of Sunday school, also, Hamilton's influence remained strong. Anderson described her favorite teacher as "the quiet person. If you looked around and saw her looking at you, you knew you did something. You don't know what you did, but you were prepared to straighten up. And yet she was a very pleasant, sweet, soft person."[15]

Members of Cego Baptist Church voiced similar praise for Lorene Wittner, who taught all ages but especially enjoyed children in first to sixth grades. Wittner recalled that she taught Sunday school at the Cego church "all of my life, ever since I married," including the first nineteen years of marriage when she still belonged to the Methodist church. Dora Miller remembered that Wittner "always had something for us to do," including Bible drills, where pupils learned the books of the Bible and how to locate specific scripture verses in a matter of seconds. Wittner's class met within the small space created by curtains partitioning off the sanctuary, and sometimes a child's attention strayed from the lesson to activities on the curtain's other side. Dora Miller reported that one look

GOSHEN CEMETERY, HARRISON

GRAVE MARKER, MOUNT MORIAH CEMETERY, RIESEL

from Wittner was all it took to restore a child's attention. Wittner herself remembered a time it took more than a look. One morning a boy in her class, who happened to be the preacher's son, propped his feet up on the table. Wittner told him to take his feet down, but he did not move. Next, she tried shame, asking, "What would it look like if we all propped up our feet?" Receiving no response, the teacher "reached over and bopped him one." She immediately feared his parents' reaction. "Oh, I really suffered," she recalled, "but you know what? That kid took his feet off and I never had any more trouble after that."

Having relatives for teachers multiplied the chances that parents would hear of their child's untoward words or actions during Sunday school. For many years, Thomas Herrington was the lone pupil in his aunt Allie Hardcastle's Sunday-school class at Cego Baptist Church. Years later, at the same church, Herrington's young nephew Edward listened to his teacher, who was also his grandmother, explain the meaning of the bread and the wine. At the mention of wine, Edward told the class, "You know what? My daddy drank all my mama's wine!" The teacher-grandmother knew that the doctor had prescribed two tablespoons of wine daily to her daughter-in-law and son to help them gain weight, but the facts did not lessen the amusement she enjoyed upon the boy's statement. What the other children told their anti-drinking Baptist parents about Edward's remarks is unknown, but his mother heard about it from her mother-in-law at dinnertime following the church service. "She couldn't wait till we all got up to the table to tell that, what Edward had said," Norma Herrington recounted.[16]

For most rural churches, the pastor was the "mortar that kept it together," as Louise Yows, a lifelong member of St. John Lutheran Church, put it.[17] The crucial role of pastor, however, was usually a part-time, nonresident one among open-country churches. Congregations and pastors worked together to solve problems of distance and funding. From their beginnings, Methodist and Baptist congregations often shared a building, with itinerant preachers from the two denominations rotating Sundays in the pulpit. At other times, the pastor of one denomination served both, which sometimes created problems for church and pastor. In 1937, William Gardiner Ellis became pastor of the joint Baptist-Methodist church in Leroy, and in 1945, he added the pastorate of the union church in Birome, all the while holding a full-time secular job in Waco. For fifty-five years Ellis led Leroy Church, where, he confessed, he favored baptism by immersion, which annoyed his Methodist members. Conversely, his tolerance of Methodists caused Baptists from other churches to question his loyalty. Through the years, when other Baptist churches interviewed Ellis in view of a call to their vacant pulpits, he felt, "I could never get out of there because I was striped. I was striped; I will admit that. I'm still quite broadminded. I have a very good feeling that there'll be Methodist people in heaven just as well as Baptist people in heaven."[18]

Rural Baptist churches often hired ministerial students from Baylor University in Waco or Southwestern Baptist Theological Seminary in Fort Worth to travel to their communities for Sunday services. Reliance on students to fill their pulpits meant churches faced a pastor turnover every two to three years. In the fifty-two years from 1932 to 1984, Liberty Hill Baptist Church had thirty-one pastors, mostly students. One pastor stayed only three months, and the longest any pastor stayed was three years. Seminarians from Fort Worth and students from Waco traveled by train into Moody or bus to Eddy on Saturday, stayed with a host family overnight, preached on Sunday, and returned to school on Sunday night or Monday morning.[19]

Cego Baptist Church also relied heavily on student pastors. "We've always considered ourselves more or less a training church," explained Lorene Wittner, "and we expected them to go on to bigger and greater things, and most of them have." Some student pastors remained in the memories of church members long after they left because of their zeal for service. Wittner recalled a student pastor who had no money to donate to the Lottie Moon Christmas Offering for foreign missions. Wittner's husband and another church leader carried the young pastor around the countryside in a truck so that he could cut down mistletoe to sell in town to raise the funds for his missions offering. Edith McKee remembered fondly another student pastor who took the time to visit the entire church membership and several of their neighbors in Cego in their homes every month.[20]

In addition to being the first church served by many young pastors, a rural church was often the last church served by an older pastor with a lifetime of experience. Following its fifty-two year stretch as a training ground for student pastors, Liberty Hill Baptist Church hired a retired pastor who served the church past his eighty-third birthday. Albert J. Martin, who had served Liberty Hill in the early 1930s at the beginning of his ministry, returned to pastor there full-time from 1984 to

ELM MOTT CEMETERY, ELM MOTT

1990. Although up in years, Reverend Martin offered his time to teach Sunday school in addition to preaching the Sunday morning service. When necessary, he also took the accompanist's place at the piano. In 1993, Charles Brinkmeyer became the second retired army chaplain to fill the pastorate for St. John Lutheran Church, at Coryell City. Brinkmeyer's assignment was "Sunday plus one," meaning he worked through all the church activities scheduled on Sundays plus one other day during the week.[21]

In more recent years, most rural pastors were bivocational, holding full-time jobs in addition to their ministry to the church. In 1993, John Hogan, who worked full-time as a City of Waco engineering technician, became pastor of Liberty Hill Baptist Church. He maintained a busy schedule of nursing home and hospital visitation, Wednesday evening prayer meetings, and full Sunday services, including leading congregational singing with his guitar. Hogan felt called to the ministry as an adult a few years after returning to Waco from military service during the Vietnam War. He worked full-time, learning engineering technology on the job, and spent his free time preaching in prisons before Liberty Hill invited him as pastor. His experience at the church was his first in a rural setting, and he took quickly to the congregation. "We have a great bunch of people out here," he explained, adding "I'll be here till they run me off." Hogan's only frustration with bivocational ministry was having "a lot I want to do but not enough time to do it." Camaraderie among other bivocational pastors in the area encouraged Hogan. For Thanksgiving and Easter and for fifth-Sunday song services, Liberty Hill teamed with churches in Bruceville and Eddy, also served by pastors with full-time jobs in addition to their pastorates.[22]

Roosevelt Fields sold life insurance full-time but dedicated Sundays and Wednesdays to his pastoral ministry at Goshen Cumberland Presbyterian Church in America (CPCA). For several years Fields also served a CPCA congregation in Bosque County, a fifty-mile drive from the Goshen church. Lawrence G. Felice, pastor of St. Paul United Church of Christ, in Falls County, was a full-time professor of sociology at Baylor University. Felice grew up St. Louis, Missouri, in the Evangelical and Reformed denomination and earned a degree from its Eden Seminary. In the mid-1980s, while on the Baylor faculty, he offered his services to the United Church of Christ's South Central Conference to pastor a congregation on an interim basis. He explained, "I wanted to give something back to the denomination that earlier had nurtured me." He became interim pastor

DOUBLE DOORS, COMPTON METHODIST CHURCH, NORTHWEST McLENNAN COUNTY

at the historic St. Paul church and moved into the parsonage. More than fifteen years later, he was still interim pastor there while, technically but not literally, the church sought a permanent pastor.[23]

In other cases, churches shared a minister between them. Pastors serving St. Peter's German Evangelical Church outside the town of West began a joint ministry with St. Paul's church upon its founding in 1900 in the rural community of Gerald. The pastor alternated Sundays between the two churches. To secure for themselves the advantages of a resident pastor, the congregation at St. Paul's built a parsonage for ministers serving the joint charge. Following World War II, improved roads made it possible for the pastor to travel between the churches in a timely manner on Sunday mornings, so the pastor preached at both churches every week. In 1966, St. Peter's church left the countryside and merged with the First Presbyterian Church in West to form First United Church of West. By the 1980s, the two churches were unable to find full-time ministers to accept their joint charge, so they hired a series of doctoral students from Baylor University's Department of Religion. These young men were mostly Baptists, and they complied in varying degrees with doctrines and ordinances of the United Church of Christ. One student pastor refused to conduct infant baptisms and to recite the Apostle's Creed, but another joined the United Church of Christ and sought training at its seminary.[24]

INTERIOR, COMPTON METHODIST CHURCH, NORTHWEST McLENNAN COUNTY

As St. Paul's approached its one-hundredth anniversary, its first woman pastor, Jane Lovett, held the joint West-Gerald charge. Pastoring two churches was only half of Lovett's vocation. She was full-time nursing home chaplain for Central Texas Senior Ministry in Waco and on-call chaplain for Scott & White Hospital in Temple. The West-Gerald charge was Lovett's second joint appointment; from 1984 to 1989, she served United Methodist churches at Riesel and Meier Settlement. The churches at West and Gerald met separately every Sunday until a fifth Sunday occurred during a month, when they shared one service. They also met jointly during Lent, for Ash Wednesday, Maundy Thursday, and Good Friday services.

Experience taught Lovett flexibility; she reported, "I've learned in being in ministry in twenty years that you don't have to get uptight if everything doesn't go perfectly." During one four-week period, from August to September, 1998, Lovett's calendar included confirmation of four young women, an infant baptism, a wedding, and a funeral, in addition to the special afternoon service of installation, which gave her pastoral standing in the North Texas Association of the United Church of Christ. On Sundays, she drove to West from her home on the other side of Waco for the 9:30 A.M. worship service, where she led music, preached, and, on the first Sunday of each month, served communion. After staying long enough to greet the small congregation, Lovett drove about nine miles to St. Paul's, Gerald, arriving less than ten minutes before its 11:00 A.M. worship services. St. Paul's lay leaders knew the routine well and prepared the sanctuary for the service. While Lovett donned her clerical robes, a church member lit the altar candles and the sexton rang the bell. Once the service began, Lovett often found it necessary to adjust quickly to sudden changes from the planned format. Surprises might include the unscheduled absence of the pianist, requiring a change from the hymns printed in the weekly bulletin to ones the substitute pianist could play. She asked congregational leaders to place notes on the pulpit with any last-minute information she needed to know for the welcome and announcements.

Lovett learned to adjust to the distinctive personalities of her two churches. At West, the smaller church, the congregation sang from old, traditional hymnals, while the Gerald church adopted new denominational hymnals. Gradually, she introduced new programs in the churches, including vacation Bible school and Lenten week Bible study. She initiated Holy Week services for the entire West community and association-wide summer worship services at the Master's Workshop, the regional

BOSQUEVILLE UNITED METHODIST CHURCH, BOSQUEVILLE

denominational camp. To make her sermons particularly memorable, Lovett included interpretive dance, and once she dressed as the mother of Jesus and delivered her message in first person.[25]

Carol Grant Gibson held a full-time pastoral charge at Bracks Chapel United Methodist Church in Waco and a bimonthly charge at Springhill United Methodist, about fifteen miles away. Her home was in Temple, Texas, thirty miles away, where her husband was also a full-time pastor. Springhill held worship services on second and fourth Sundays each month. Following an 8:30 A.M. Sunday-school hour, worship services began at Springhill at 9:45 A.M. Pastor Gibson completed her sermon at Springhill and drove immediately to Waco in time to enter the sanctuary about forty-five minutes into the worship service, initiated at 11:00 A.M. by lay leaders. In spite of the demands of three churches, two as pastor and one as pastor's wife, Gibson managed to make hospital visits and meet counseling requests. Ernestine Anderson testified, "When her members are ill, she's there. When that call comes into the hospital, she's there. If you have a problem and if you tell her you need her, she's there."[26]

Since its beginning in 1922, St. Joseph's Catholic Church, Elk, shared a priest, initially with Assumption Parish in Waco and, after 1942, with St. Martin's Catholic Church, Tours. Father Isidore Rozychi, appointed to St. Martin's and St. Joseph's in 1987, felt that his schedule "short-changed" the families at Elk. At Tours, he held mass at eight o'clock every weekday morning, and to accommodate people who worked on Sundays, he also held mass on Saturday evenings. At Elk, he celebrated mass on weekdays only on the evenings of special feast days. On Sunday mornings, in all seasons, he rode a motorcycle eleven miles from the Tours rectory to Elk to conduct early mass, followed by a rushed return to Tours for morning mass there. Although Sunday mornings found him busy at the altar of two different churches, he confessed, "I feel sometimes like I never go to church, you know it? I'm going to say I'm presiding. I go to Elk and I can't stay long if we have a reception or something else because I've got church here, so I run to the hall for about two minutes and say hello and come back here. I just get here by the time church starts, so I always start late here, and I'm out of breath when I get here. And all of a sudden I go, change, and put on my vestments, and I go show, you know it?"

On the other hand, Rozychi saw great reward in the opportunity to know the families in the small church community. In the rural church, he said, "You become involved with them personally, with their family. You baptize their children, you see these kids make their first communion,

CANAAN BAPTIST CHURCH, NEAR CRAWFORD

INTERIOR, CANAAN BAPTIST CHURCH, NEAR CRAWFORD

confirmation, you see these same kids get married, and sometimes you see those same kids die. You're with them through the happy moments and sad moments." In addition to his spiritual responsibilities at two churches, Father Rozychi organized twice-monthly senior adult bus trips to Louisiana casinos. He served as chaplain for the Waco Police Department and provided mass for the Catholic hospital and assisted living centers in Waco. Then, on Friday nights every fall for twenty-five years, he officiated at high school football games throughout the eastern half of Texas.[27]

In the 1920s and throughout the Great Depression, rural pastors received little if any regular salary. During the depression, one rural church initiated a systematic method for giving that called for each young person to contribute a dime per week and each adult, a quarter. Many farm families, large ones especially, sometimes found it hard to give a weekly offering, so some churches sent representatives to members' homes to collect funds. Mount Olive Missionary Baptist Church, Downsville, organized the congregation into tribes, with captains who were each responsible for visiting the members assigned to their tribe and collecting money to pay the preacher. Fred Douglas Tucker recalled that his family could often afford to donate only a dime at a time. The pastor accepted whatever the congregation could pay.[28]

When J. K. Rystad began serving as pastor of Our Savior's Lutheran Church, the church set a figure of five hundred dollars for his annual salary, but in reality the church had no operating budget. Once or twice a year, several men collected donations for the pastor's salary from other church members and what they collected was the annual salary, whether or not it reached five hundred dollars. Cash was much less forthcoming than hams, chickens, and garden produce. Likewise, when the longtime church treasurer of Cego Baptist Church visited members to collect the pastor's salary, he accepted chickens or anything else he could sell to obtain cash. Dora Miller recalled that her mother once donated canned peaches to help cover the pastor's salary. Sunday offerings also supplemented the pastor's salary, and one Sunday when the donations fell short of the full salary, according to Thomas Herrington, the treasurer took funds from his personal bank account as a loan to the church. Longtime Sunday-school secretary Edith Bridger McKee recalled many Sundays when she just handed over to the preacher all the loose change and bills received in the morning's offering. Parishioners at St. Joseph's Catholic Church, Elk, held picnics and bingo games every July to raise funds for both building upkeep and the priest's salary. Regular offerings sometimes provided only ten dollars per week, but the annual sale of fried chicken or barbecue dinners and proceeds from bingo games augmented that amount.[29]

Pastors in rural churches supplemented their salaries in creative ways. According to Lonnie Graves, one of the early Baptist ministers among the African American community in northern Falls County was also a teacher in the local school, and another one of the early Methodist ministers led a community band, complete with bass horn, cornets, clarinets, and a drum. Other pastors

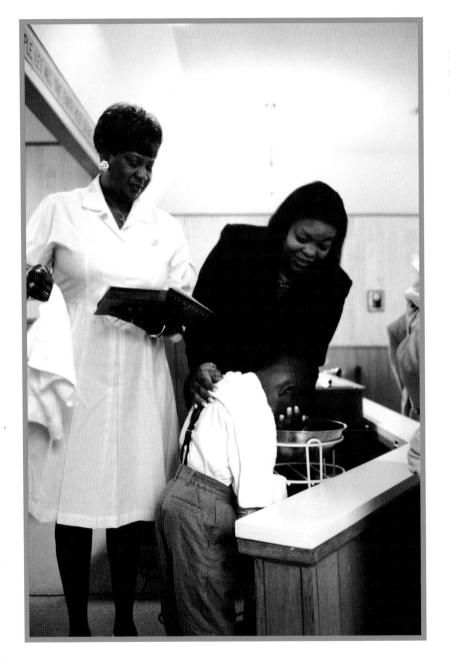

BAPTISM,
SPRINGHILL UNITED
METHODIST
CHURCH, RIESEL

farmed, like most of their parishioners. Reverend Hogan Guy served Cedar Grove Baptist Church, Satin, for more than thirty years, from about 1927 to the early 1960s. Graves recalled Pastor Guy as a farmer who "didn't depend upon the church to take care of him." Katherine Guy, the wife of Hogan Guy's nephew and a member of the Cedar Grove church since the age of thirteen, stated that families normally placed only a quarter in the offering plate each Sunday; the pastor, therefore, "would take whatever we gave him and sometimes he would give it back to the church." She remembered that Hogan Guy had no car to cross the river to reach the church, so he pulled his shoes off, walked across the river when it was low, and then put on his shoes again after wiping the mud from his feet. Pastor Guy's example of financial independence inspired others in the community. Graves testified, "The people looked at the Rev. Hogan Guy as something, as some kind of person who stood on his own, who would stand shoulder to shoulder with the people in Marlin or whoever, even though he was not educated."[30]

In 1894, when Heinrich Engelbrecht gave Canaan Baptist Church land for a church, cemetery, and parsonage, he also included adjoining acreage for pastors to raise crops, plus acreage for pasture to support some cattle for additional income. Pastor George Hege, who served in the mid-1920s, became known as a perfectionist who demanded excellence from both his choir and his garden, where he hoed admirable straight rows and grew healthy herbs in addition to staple vegetables. Pastor Cornelius Gossen raised a garden and kept a milk cow, chickens, and hogs to provide food for his family through the Great Depression. After Gossen left, Canaan's pastors farmed their allotted acreage less and less, and the church eventually sold the acreage to help finance the cemetery's perpetual care program.[31]

Ernestine Anderson believed that each pastor in the history of Springhill Methodist Church was the right person for the church's needs at the time they served. The most effective pastors, she thought, were ones who turned the congregation gently toward new ideas and ways of doing things. Heavy-handed authority met resistance among a people for whom church was the one safe place outside home where they could take a strongly independent stand. "A lot of times that old heritage of the past that includes that segregation, that slavery, all that stuff, comes out," Anderson explained. "You don't have to be born into something to remember what your people tell you that they suffered through."

Anderson cited S. A. Keesee, who served Springhill during the 1940s, as the builder of both the church and its people, literally and figuratively. First, Keesee convinced his congregation that with hard work and sacrifice they could improve their church building and grounds. With new physical facilities accomplished and a seed of confidence planted, Keesee then began applying the principle of economic independence to home life. More than fifty years after the fact, Anderson remembered Keesee's message to a congregation economically bound by the crop-lien system: "God wants the best for you, and God equipped you with the knowledge of things that you can do for yourself. He will help you, but he's not going to do it for you. You have to have the initiative. And he did not mean for you to stay in bondage." Keesee raised the questions, "Why don't you have your own land? Why don't you have your own home? Why don't you have the say of where your children go and do? Why do you have to get permission from others?"

As a pastor in good standing in the community, Keesee had access to bank loans unavailable to other African Americans in the segregated South, so he obtained a loan to purchase more than one hundred acres of land along Mount Moriah Road, near the church, with the intention of building a home on one parcel and selling the remaining parcels to church members willing to take the giant step to land ownership. Anderson recalled Keesee's saying, "If you will do it, I will stand for the land. I will go to the man, and I will contract for this land. You tell me how much each of you want. And if you don't pay it, I have to pay it." The pastor's willingness to assume such a risk when his own income depended on the offerings of a congregation of poor tenant farmers helped sway about five families to buy land and build their own houses. Fathers supplemented their income with jobs at the cotton gin or oil presses or drove the new tractors that began to replace mules and plows on farms on which they were formerly tenants. Mothers all along Mount Moriah Road took daytime housekeeping jobs in Waco. By the time the Methodists reassigned Keesee to other service in the denomination, not only did Springhill have a new, updated sanctuary, but five of its families were new landowners, living in houses built by their own hands with their pastor's skilled help.[32]

Faithful pastors of open-county churches recognized the importance of their roles, but understood well that their churches belonged to a higher authority. Pastor John Hogan of Liberty Hill Baptist Church believed that his rural church persisted in spite of frequent pastor turnovers because of the consistency of God's love. "The thing is you can't put your finger on any one person," he said. "Look how many times the pastor has changed. It had to be God that kept it alive all of these years and that keeps it growing and keeps people interested and involved in it." Roosevelt Fields, pastor of Goshen Cumberland Presbyterian Church in America, likewise credited its survival for more than 130 years to a faithful God. "You know," he said, "there was some times I imagine that they didn't know how they was going to even get by, but I believe it was just trusting in God is what gave them that endurance to be able to hold onto God's unchanging hand."[33]

CHAPTER 5

Facing Change

"IN EVERY CHANGE, HE FAITHFUL WILL REMAIN."

—*Be Still, My Soul*

AS TIME PASSED AND DISTANCE INCREASED between successive generations and their rural roots, open-country congregations in Central Texas with a will to survive began broadening their reach beyond familial and cultural foundations. Denominations responded to the longevity of their rural churches in various ways, some providing authoritative structure and others encouraging increasing autonomy and self-sufficiency. Locating pastoral leadership for rural congregations reached a critical state. Traditional values associated with rural life, including the centrality of the church, faced complex challenges in contemporary society, requiring congregations to adapt new strategies for survival. In every decision it faced, the rural church found itself caught between retaining cherished traditions and embracing new ideas.

Rural depopulation left few young people in open-country churches. Families at St. Paul's United Church of Christ, Gerald, retired from farming by the end of the twentieth century, and Pastor Jane

PASTOR JANE LOVETT, ST. PAUL'S UNITED CHURCH OF CHRIST, GERALD

Lovett estimated that the majority of members then were more than seventy years old. In the early 1990s, St. Paul's, Gerald, went through a period when only older adults filled its pews on Sunday mornings. In less than ten years, however, several young people who had moved away for education, job training, and marriage began having children of their own and, although they lived in Waco, Robinson, and Lorena, they gradually returned to the old family church. Children attending Sunday school numbered only six, but even so, Lovett explained, having children there added "a point of stability in the midst of everything changing." For the generations, she said, the church "represents something stable in life and it's the reminder that there is something that will carry you through even in the midst of change." Albert Leuschner noted the change made by the presence of children in the congregation: "And now it's great. Every Sunday you're going to hear something besides the preacher's voice. So that's a good sign, I would think."[1]

St. John Evangelical Lutheran Church, in Coryell City, reached its centennial in 1989 having few children and mostly older adults on Sunday mornings. Lifelong member Louise Yows counted about twenty-five widows among the worshippers one Sunday morning, composing about half the congregation that day. St. John's pastor, Charles Brinkmeyer, estimated that the average age of his active members was sixty. On Sunday mornings the pastor might greet the eldest members in German, their childhood language. Many of the younger adult members were husbands and wives of St. John members with backgrounds in denominations other than Lutheran. Brinkmeyer applauds such "blending," and, to accommodate those from other traditions, he continued the practice begun by his predecessor of alternating worship styles each week. First and third Sundays of the month are traditional Lutheran services, with communion and a liturgical program following the Lutheran Book of Worship. Lutheran hymns sung on those weeks originated in the nineteenth century, Brinkmeyer said, noting that each hymn is a sermon, with a theological message and stately tune. In contrast, on second and fourth Sundays, St. John's holds what Brinkmeyer labeled "a Baptist service," in which the congregation worships in a contemporary praise style, using an American gospel hymnal. The pastor explained that people left services on those weeks humming, evidence to him that "catchy melodies" might stay with a worshipper longer than Old World hymns.[2]

Commingling traditions signals for some congregations the loss of their distinctive ethnic flavor. Albert Leuschner, of St. Paul's United Church of Christ in Gerald, admitted his reluctance

CHURCH SIGN, TOURS

toward community outreach. "If you're going to really accept other people in, then your heritage is going to change," he feared. Newcomers faced an invisible barrier within his church, he said, where "they're liable to be in but be an outsider even though the people are friendly and acceptable." To ensure its future, Pastor Jane Lovett encouraged St. Paul's, Gerald, to reach beyond its core families to neighbors moving into the area without prior connections to the church. Having served in other rural congregations, however, Lovett recognized, "It can be intimidating to new people to come in and see all these folks with this extended family, and the brothers and the sisters and the cousins and the aunts, the uncles, and all of a sudden, everybody's related and you feel like, Where's my place?" Sunday-school teacher for the adult class, Wilma Altus Richter hoped St. Paul's, Gerald, might open a daycare center or after-school play center for local children in the area, but hers was a lone voice among her fellow church members.[3]

Insularity was common among open-country churches with strong ethnic backgrounds whose leadership remained in the hands of a few families from their beginnings more than a hundred years ago. Carol Grant Gibson, pastor of Springhill United Methodist Church, encouraged those "stout, longtime, older members, who pretty much hold things together" to accommodate the younger, city-raised generation, with the goal of "trying to get them rooted in that same fashion, so that [the church] does have a future and one that will last beyond their lifetimes." In addition, Gibson hoped to inspire the church to stretch beyond their kin, emphasizing a program of "outreach to reach those who do not belong, who are not attached, to find some way of enticing them to come here to keep this particular church going." "What she's saying," explained Ernestine Anderson, "is in this small community there are people around us on this road that attend no churches. They don't participate in anything. If you ask the church members, Springhill members, about these people, we don't know anything about them." Anderson, whose roots at Springhill extend back four generations, embraced the pastor's agenda, admitting, "If you get too set in your ways that you're not flexible enough for new innovations to come in, new ideas, new changes, just because we have never done it that way, don't try to do it, you can also destroy yourself, too."[4]

At two Falls County United Church of Christ congregations, both named St. Paul, efforts to push the church beyond its own walls failed. "Most of the members don't want to grow," confessed Lawrence G. Felice, pastor at St. Paul, outside Marlin. "This has been their church, they like it the

HYMN BOARD, ST. MARTIN'S CATHOLIC CHURCH, TOURS

way it is, they don't want to see any change. They're willing to let the doors close when enough die." By 2000, his church membership rolls listed seventy-three people, with an average worship attendance of twenty. St. Paul's, Cego, listed only thirty-five members in 2000 and the pastor, Jeffrey W. Taylor, reported a regular attendance of about a dozen. Taylor summarized the situation facing his congregation: "The twentieth century, in its last half, has bypassed Cego. The twenty-first will probably forget about it altogether." With population loss, commercialization of agriculture, and

the last store's closing, Taylor claimed, "No rational person would try to plan a new church in Cego; they would go somewhere else."[5]

Typical of the other few members remaining in her church, eighty-two-year-old Corine Niesen Miller still lived in the home where she was born and still attended St. Paul's, Cego, where she and her six siblings received baptism as infants. With three sisters physically unable to attend services and two brothers living far away, and with none of their children remaining in the Cego area, the only Niesen descendants attending St. Paul's were Corine Miller and her daughter Helen, who drove to the country from Waco every weekend to be in church with her mother. One new couple, who lived weekdays in Spring, Texas, 150 miles south, and weekends at their ranch near Cego, joined the church in recent years. Otherwise, new families in the area knew virtually nothing about the white frame church in their neighborhood. One member explained the church's dilemma, saying, "I think sometimes, Well, should we take the responsibility to go and meet them? When new people move in, in some respects you think that that's the neighborly thing to do. But yet, on the other hand, in today's world you're never sure whether you want to meet the person that's next door. In some cases, it's better to not know, and it's sad that the world is like that now, because it is nice to have community and friends close by."[6]

As newcomers repopulated former farm lands in the late twentieth century, creating bedroom communities, many open-country churches survived low points in membership and experienced rebirth. By 1998, descendants of the four original families who in 1910 organized Liberty Hill Baptist Church had dwindled to less than a half dozen people, most in frail health. The rolling prairie visible from the hilltop church, located just a few miles west of Interstate 35, attracted new families, however, who wanted to raise their children in the country and educate them in small school districts. Newcomers, like the Holt family who moved into the area in 1985, built new homes, leased fields and pastures to farmers and stock raisers, and commuted to Waco and Temple for work. While the Holts' home was under construction, they received a visit and personal invitation to church from Bernice Porter Bostick Weir, a Liberty Hill member since the 1930s. The Holts and other newcomers stepped into many church leadership roles once held by Weir's generation. Lynn Holt explained, "We don't have

SIGN, LIBERTY GROVE, NORTHERN McLENNAN COUNTY

many that have any ties to past members. Most of them have just proved that they want to work in the church when they come in. We have a lot of people who are really good about not just being pew-sitters and want to get up and do something for the church, so we really never had to go begging to do any job." News of the church's regeneration inspired many former members living elsewhere to return to Liberty Hill for annual homecomings and send financial support to assist the church.[7]

Trinity Lutheran Church, east of Riesel, likewise survived in open country as its neighbors changed from farmers to commuters. Pastor Alfred Gallmeier estimated that less than a half dozen "true farmers" remained in the congregation by 2001, although several "hobby farmers" who had other incomes from urban jobs were in the church. At its peak in the late 1930s, the church had 630 baptized members and 440 communicant members. The number of baptized members declined to a low of 200 and gradually returned to about 350 members. For eighty-one years, from 1884 to 1965, Trinity operated a parochial day school. In 2001, the church had both a daycare center and an after-school program to accommodate working families in its vicinity. Gallmeier considered the church's focus on children as its hope for the future. "If we don't have anything to meet the needs of the people, then there is no future for us, but if we become a part of the growing community, meeting the needs that they have, yes, I think it will grow."[8]

Along with rural population changes, the latter half of the twentieth century brought transitions in denominational practice, as was the case for Roman Catholics following Vatican II, and in denominational structure and doctrine, as experienced through unions of various Protestant groups. As crossroads villages disappeared, denominations governed from above encouraged consolidation of small churches when necessary and provided joint pastoral assignments for congregations still viable. For autonomous churches, freedom to direct their own course afforded the opportunity to keep going, if they so chose, even through changing times. Some rural autonomous churches, however, found themselves unable to fill their pastorates and increasingly distanced from their denominations on theological and social issues.

Strong loyalty to the Catholic faith continued for rural parishioners, but they noted vast changes in worship ritual since the 1960s and Vatican II. Services formerly held in Latin were now

ELM MOTT CEMETERY, ELM MOTT

in English; the priest faced the congregation rather than the altar when performing the mass; altar helpers no longer wore the traditional black cassock, and girls as well as boys now assisted the priest; hymn singing became a part of the worship; and children were confirmed at an older age than in days gone by. Experiencing the mass in English rather than Latin was the greatest change noted in a lifetime of Catholicism for Walter Dulock, who was altar boy for twenty years. For Evelyn Cunningham and her husband, Robert Cunningham, the greatest change was among the priests, with the "old school" priest being strict and formal and the "new school" priest being friendlier and more appealing to young people. Walter Dulock described the way Father Isidore Rozychi warmed St. Joseph's congregation before the sermon: "Every Sunday morning before he has his sermon he tells a little joke, and then when he has his sermon he ties his joke in with his sermon. It kind of loosens you up. He gets your attention when he tells his joke, and then he comes up with his sermon and ties it." Another recent change in St. Joseph's services called for greater participation by the congregation. Evelyn Cunningham compared the past and present worship services: "Then you didn't sing or anything in church. It was very quiet. But now in this church, now we sing. You'd think we were in a Protestant church. We just sing out like all get-out."

During the late 1990s, the young descendants of Elk's Czech Catholics still attended weekly religion classes, many driven by their parents to the country from their homes in town to receive spiritual training at the site of their family's roots. Rather than catechism classes taught by nuns, they attended a program called CCD, Confraternity of Christian Doctrine, taught by parent volunteers using brightly illustrated materials. They attended classes once a week during the school year, being confirmed usually at age fourteen. Longtime members of St. Joseph's who received the much more rigorous church training of the past bemoaned the lack of loyalty to the Elk church among recent confirmands. "Once they get them out of confirmation," explained Evelyn Cunningham, "they go off to somewhere else. They don't come back. What scares me is that they're not living here, but through Grandpa and Grandma they come for the classes and then they're not here for Sunday services."[9]

The United Methodist Church, created in 1968 with the union of the Methodist Church and the Evangelical United Brethren Church, works through a hierarchy of regional jurisdictions and area conferences to set educational standards for pastors, provide financial resources, and train members in church matters. The denominational authority structure affords greater security for the

BEHIND GOSHEN CUMBERLAND PRESBYTERIAN CHURCH IN AMERICA, HARRISON

LIBERTY HILL BAPTIST CHURCH, NEAR MOODY

survival of its small churches, according to Ernestine Anderson. Being small in membership did not prevent her church, Springhill United Methodist, from active participation in either the former all-black West Texas Conference or the current Central Texas Conference, which absorbed the segregated conference in 1970. Former Springhill pastors, S. A. Keesee and E. C. Purnell, moved from service at the church into the office of district superintendent in the West Texas Conference. After 1970, Springhill remained active in the Waco District of the Central Texas Conference, participating often in its church leadership and business training programs. Through the year, Springhill received welcomed visits from its district superintendent, who served on-call to minister to churches and individual members. Because it shared a pastor with Bracks Chapel United Methodist Church in Waco, Springhill and its sister church held between them one laity vote and one pastoral vote in the annual conference meeting, a week-long session of daytime business meetings and evening worship services to which the two churches sent local delegates on alternating years. The annual conference assigned pastors to their charges each June and provided information to delegates on matters of church policy to be discussed in the triennial general conferences. In addition to attendance on alternate years at the annual conference, Springhill's five lay leaders represented the church at other district and conference meetings and carried news and issues back to the congregation for discussion. The relationship between the small rural church and its district was strong enough to allow Anderson to profess, "For me it makes me feel secure. It makes me feel a part of the whole global United Methodist and I'm not just a piecemeal person."

Denominational support continued forthcoming for Springhill United Methodist Church in providing resources, training, and a stable pastorate. In 2000, the Central Texas Conference renewed Rev. Carol Gibson's sixth annual joint appointment to Bracks Chapel and Springhill. Even if the Methodists ceased sending a pastor to Springhill, the church would survive as long as the families remained, according to one member. Glenda Garrett claimed, "If the conference decided that they wouldn't send someone, I don't think any of us could ever let the doors of Springhill close. It will continue even if it goes back to the old days of give us a song and a prayer and we'll celebrate the Lord just with the two that's here."[10]

Locally autonomous, Southern Baptist churches voluntarily aligned on the regional level with associations and on the statewide level with the Baptist General Convention of Texas (BGCT). At the end of the twentieth century, despite the high visibility of its large metropolitan congregations, the BGCT reported that 45 percent of its churches remained in areas of less than 2,500 population. Over the years, the BGCT sponsored various improvement programs to assist rural churches, with a particular emphasis on evangelism and outreach. During his two years as pastor of Liberty Hill Baptist Church, Parma G. Newman led the congregation to participate with 707 other Texas churches in the 1966 BGCT Church Development Program, which provided guidance,

ST. PAUL'S UNITED CHURCH OF CHRIST, CEGO

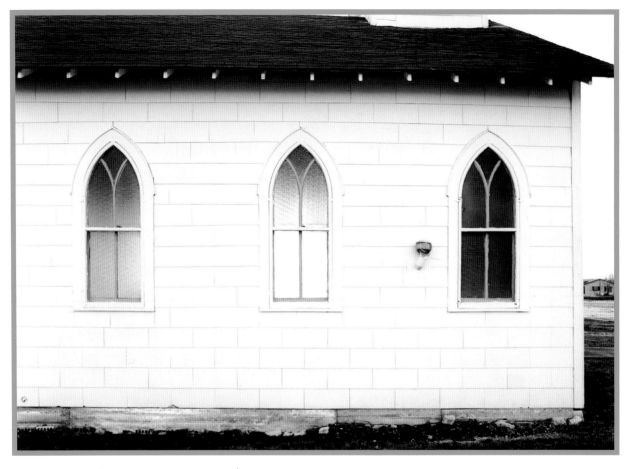

THREE WINDOWS, ST. PAUL'S UNITED CHURCH OF CHRIST, CEGO

materials, and recognition to encourage churches to set goals for evangelizing their neighborhoods and increasing their support for worldwide missions. Before 1965, Liberty Hill had reduced its program to Sunday school and worship services only, but during the first year of the development program it added Training Union, Woman's Missionary Union, Brotherhood, and a Sunday School Extension Department to serve members unable to attend on Sunday mornings. Also under the state program, the church conducted a neighborhood survey to identify prospective members, through which it discovered twenty-two persons more than nine years of age who were members of no church and twenty-six persons who were Baptists without local affiliation. Within a years' time, Liberty Hill baptized five and enlisted eight of its neighbors. The pastor instituted a regular schedule of visiting church members to discuss the needs of the church and community, and the church held a week-long revival.

Liberty Hill Baptist remained a strong presence in southern McLennan County thirty years later. In 1998, when the BGCT's Waco Baptist Association held its annual Sunday-school clinic, all of Liberty Hill's Sunday-school teachers, all its deacons, and its pastor attended. Pastor John Hogan explained, however, that as a bivocational pastor, he gave priority to local church matters over associational affairs. "The church comes first and the needs of the church come first," he said. Hogan reserved vacation and personal time off from his secular job for attending to special needs of Liberty Hill members, including funerals, weddings, hospital calls, and mission trips, rather than for attendance at state and national denominational meetings. Until 2001, the church remained neutral in the doctrinal controversies affecting the relationship between the Southern Baptist Convention and the BGCT. "We stay out of that," Hogan said in 1998. "My job is to pastor this church. It's not to be embroiled in a big controversy over this or that. If it doesn't have to do with the Lord Jesus Christ, I'm going to just stay out of it and let somebody else fight that battle. I've got my hands full. We do pray that God would give them guidance, but I have to take care of business here first." Nevertheless, in April 2001, Liberty Hill joined the recently organized Southern Baptists of Texas Convention, a state group supportive of conservative stances adopted by the national convention and opposed by the BGCT.[11]

Members of rural United Church of Christ congregations also reported ways in which autonomy helped ensure their preservation. Between 1881 and 1904 ten German-language Evangelical

congregations appeared in towns and villages within a thirty-mile radius of Waco. In 1934, the national denomination under which these churches operated, the Evangelical Synod of North America, merged with the Reformed Church in the United States, composed of other German-language churches sharing a mild Calvinist theology and locally autonomous organization. The Central Texas congregations took the title of the new denomination, the Evangelical and Reformed Church, known casually as E&R. The E&R churches around Waco saw little effect from the 1934 merger, which one member termed "a happy wedding." In contrast, in 1961, when the Evangelical and Reformed Church merged with the Congregational and Christian churches to form the United Church of Christ, they noted dramatic differences. One loyal member claimed that in that second merger "they made a mistake; they've just gone wacky." In response to the change, her church ceased sending offerings to the national body and limited its support only to the regional association. Nomenclature added to their problem. In Texas, outsiders confused the name United Church of Christ with the Churches of Christ, which grew from the nineteenth-century Campbell-Stone restorationist movement and had a strong presence throughout the state. Churches of Christ used no musical instruments in their worship services, and strangers who entered a United Church of Christ on a Sunday morning expecting a Church of Christ worship experience received an embarrassing surprise. One pastor reported, "When they come and see the organ and piano they don't stay very long. They don't stay and chat; they realize they've made a mistake."[12]

Although similarities existed in the theological stances and organizational structures of the denominations that merged to create the United Church of Christ, they differed in culture and heritage. John Hayden, a pastor and associational leader, said, "The biggest tension that we have in the churches right now is the gap between how the people sitting in the pews in rural, predominately E&R churches understand the Bible and how our leadership in Cleveland, Ohio, treats the scriptures." Nationwide, as in Central Texas, the former E&R congregations were rural agrarian or urban working-class churches. Their memberships reflected family ties maintained over several generations with a common ethnic heritage. Most held services in German until World War II. Their worship emphasized God's love and their ministry focused upon fellow church members. In contrast, the Congregational and Christian churches with which the E&R merged served mostly urban areas. These churches had an Anglo heritage dating to the Puritans, represented more economically advantaged populations, and oriented their ministries toward aggressive social action. Congregational Christian churches emphasized support for educational enterprises, while E&R churches concentrated their giving on humanitarian organizations, such as children's homes, retirement facilities, and hospitals.[13]

Within the first decade of its organizing, the United Church of Christ approved ordination of homosexuals and the use of gender-inclusive language, issues that created concern among former E&R churches, conservative by tradition. One lifelong member of a rural E&R church stated that the changes caused "a terrible identity crisis" that was both "dramatic" and "traumatic" among her congregation. Because they were autonomous, the former E&R rural churches decided which denominational policies to adopt, modify, or discard. Some individual members and pastors joined the conservative renewal movement, Biblical Witness Fellowship, created in 1978, with hopes of reforming the denomination from within.[14] Twenty years later, thirty-one UCC churches grew impatient with internal attempts to renew the denomination and formed the Evangelical Association of Reformed and Congregational Christian Churches. From its national headquarters in New Braunfels, Texas, the new organization promoted renewal through individual, autonomous congregations, which it believed "must be free to pursue evangelism and ecumenical relationships in their own area without the encumbrances of denominational barriers."[15]

Autonomy allowed United Churches of Christ to express their individuality but, according to John Hayden, also curtailed the former "connectedness of the churches, the responsibility towards one another and accountability" afforded within the synodic structure of the E&R church. The natural consequence of too much local autonomy may be, Hayden added, that "everything will just kind of unravel." On the other hand, a longtime pastor's wife and active participant in Biblical Witness Fellowship said, "As long as we can preach the gospel and carry on the message of Jesus Christ, I don't think there's any problem with doing your own thing. That's the more important thing and above all else. But above denominationalism or whatever is the message of Christ. As long as we can carry that forward I think we'll continue to be what we want to be. When that ceases, then we really don't need to be a church anyway."[16]

INTERIOR, LIBERTY HILL
BAPTIST CHURCH,
NEAR MOODY

CHURCH REGISTER, LIBERTY HILL BAPTIST CHURCH, NEAR MOODY

Pastoral leadership was a key to the endurance of rural churches, and a growing paucity of suitable pastors became the greatest threat to their futures. The pastoral shortage called for flexibility and creativity on the part of both Roman Catholic and Protestant churches. Summing up the problem in locating ministers, longtime pastor Alton H. Schwecke said, "You have to take what you can get, and sometimes it works out fine and other times it doesn't. But the full-time ministry for these little country churches is getting to be something of the past due to the economy and lack of people going into ministry."

The challenge of finding pastors for rural United Churches of Christ reflected not only geographical distance from the denominational seminary but also theological distance. From its founding in 1884 to 1907, St. Paul's Evangelical Church, Cego, shared supply pastors with like congregations in Robinson, Temple, and Waco. From the completion of the parsonage in 1907 until 1939, St. Paul's supported a resident, full-time minister and experienced its peak in membership and activity. Over the following fifty-six years, as in its early years, supply pastors and those with joint charges served as part-time pastors. Although Central Texas E&R churches saw a half dozen or more of their young men enter the ministry and attend the seminary, those native sons, like their fellow seminarians, sought pastorates among churches able to support a full-time minister. Finally, on the retirement of Paul Kluge in 1994, the church welcomed student pastors from Baylor University's doctoral program in religion. "We had a Methodist preacher and Baptist preacher. We all fit in; it didn't make no difference," explained member Albert Huber. In many ways, the student pastors from conservative church backgrounds better suited the congregation than those from the United Church of Christ seminary, which ninety-year-old Huber considered "too loose" in its theological and social stances. He said, "While we were pretty strong, they'd send you a preacher, but now we got where we didn't want none of them."[17]

Problems locating denominationally trained ministers became a problem, too, for Canaan Baptist Church in the northwestern corner of McLennan County. The congregation is one of only twenty-three churches in the entire southern tier of states remaining in the North American Baptist Conference (NABC), whose headquarters are in Illinois and seminaries in Canada and South Dakota. It is also one of the last remaining rural NABC churches in the Southern Conference. Pastor

Robert Carl Scott, who served Canaan Baptist in the mid 1990s, felt that the scarcity of NABC churches in Texas enhanced their dependence upon one another. He discovered that annual Southern Conference denominational meetings were "like a family gathering. There is an appreciation of one another. It's like seeing a long-lost friend. You want to love them, not fight with them." While pastor at Canaan, Scott, a Southern Baptist, also was a doctoral student and hospital chaplain. A century ago Canaan Baptist had a full-time pastor, a former professor at Rochester Seminary, New York, and the church kept NABC pastors until the 1970s. In the last thirty years, a succession of part-time Southern Baptists, graduate students or seminarians, filled the Canaan pastorate. "We give them good experience," observed Jerry Gauer, "and when they get through we always know we're probably going to lose them because they're going to go on to better and greater things. Usually when they leave here there's lots of tears shed."[18]

Some rural churches found pastors among women called to the ministry, and reaction to female leadership was mixed, ranging from joyful acceptance to stiff opposition. The Central Texas Conference of the United Methodist Church assigned Alice P. Sims to her first full-time pastorate at rural Springhill church in 1992, and she stayed four years. When she began work at Springhill, two longtime members, both male, ceased coming to the church, claiming they did not believe women should serve as ministers. Following Sims, the conference placed Carol Grant Gibson in a joint charge between Springhill and Bracks Chapel United Methodist Church in Waco. In the first nine years women pastored Springhill, those same two male members refused to attend, but they did not move their memberships to other churches. Upon questioning, they replied, "I'll die at Springhill. I want to be buried at Springhill. When she leaves I'll be back."[19]

One solution considered for the pastoral shortage among rural congregations was development of lay leadership. In the United Methodist Church, Roman Catholic Church, and the United Church of Christ, laypersons received training and a license to administer the sacraments and lead worship in the absence of a pastor. Barbara Williams was a certified lay leader for Springhill United Methodist Church, with authority to occupy the pulpit in the pastor's absence. At St. Joseph's Catholic Church, Elk, the deacon filled in for the priest in some sacraments, performing marriages, baptizing infants, and serving communion. Robert Gorgas, the licensed lay leader for Friedens Church, Riesel, assisted his pastor, John Hayden, and filled the pulpit for St. Paul's United Church of Christ, Cego, in a period when it was without a pastor. The North Texas Association of the United Church of Christ utilized retired pastors to train lay leaders and encouraged them to take courses at area theological schools, such as Austin Presbyterian Seminary.[20]

The path a pastor faced in leading a family-run, rural church in a new direction was a slippery one. Longtime rural church members possessed a powerful sense of ownership in the church. "It takes a certain kind of minister to be a minister for the small church and then a church that is kind of steeped in older people," said Ernestine Anderson. "They don't have to be so much older in age, but just older in the church services, that know almost every nail that went into the building. You can get what you want from people much better when you use respect and you're willing to listen, if it takes thirty minutes to say what I can say in two."

Patience paid off for rural ministers who allowed members time to warm up to new ideas. From the beginning of her work at Springhill United Methodist Church, Carol Grant Gibson cultivated friendships with lifelong members who knew "the process and the psyche of the persons there." Change at Springhill from a part-time to full-time program must begin, Gibson claimed, with a change of heart: "It's a matter of them owning it and not feeling forced into it. They kind of know it in their head and are moving toward their heart. I think it will behoove me to really continue to be prayerful and make sure that I am doing it in a manner that will encourage and not discourage." She initiated a weekly evening Bible study to help members warm to the concept of weekly church activities. One of Springhill's prominent lay leaders appreciated Gibson's style, explaining, "There are things that I know I'm supposed to do, and if the minister tries to come in and change all that around for me, it's going to make a mess for me as a lay person. There's some things that I'm supposed to do that the minister has nothing to do with, but it is part of what I do to make the whole package go."[21]

Unsuccessful attempts to promote change led to the dismissal of some rural pastors. In the 1980s, one rural pastor encouraged his congregation toward outreach to the community and improvements in church facilities. Under his leadership, the church renewed its vacation Bible school and made improvements to its building with new paint and paneling and a suspended ceiling. The pastor grew aggressive, however, in making decisions without the full approval of the church. Desiring to bring area children and young people to services, he bought a van and then asked the church to repay him for it. Later, when he scheduled a church business meeting to discuss purchasing a new piano, only six members attended, so one deacon there suggested postponement of the matter. The pastor, however, continued the meeting, an act that some members considered the last straw in a long line of "demanding" or "bossy" actions. They organized a successful petition drive to request his resignation.[22]

Pastors of churches left behind in abandoned communities led congregations whose social life no longer revolved around the local church as it had before World War II. All churches—urban and rural—experienced the consequences of a society where families engaged in multiple social activities unrelated to their spiritual lives. To attract and serve busy families, pastors promoted flexible schedules and creative programming, requiring forfeiture of traditional meeting times and long-practiced formats. Schools and communities once curtailed social events on Wednesday evenings because that was "church night" for congregations who held midweek mission groups, prayer meetings, and choir practice. But as John Hayden, moderator for the North Texas Association of the United Church of Christ, explained, "The understanding of time at church being the social gathering is gone." He said, "We compete for time. The school has things for our kids and their parents to do every day of the week, including Sunday." The only ones attending on weeknights at his church were older adults who participated in the Women's Guild and Brotherhood. When parents failed to attend the midweek meetings and bring their children, some older adults wondered, "I used to come with my mom. Why can't they do it?" The Women's Guild faced the choice of holding evening meetings to allow working women to attend or daytime meetings to accommodate older women unable to drive at night. Trying to model flexibility for his members, Hayden moved confirmation classes from Saturday to Tuesday afternoons to accommodate busy student schedules.[23]

Carol Grant Gibson encouraged Springhill United Methodist Church to shed its century-old habit of holding only bimonthly worship services in favor of weekly meetings. "If we're really wanting to grow and really are looking at our long-term standing and openness and survival even, if we're going to get new persons really to root there other than just family members being born

CHURCH SIGN, MOUNT MORIAH BAPTIST CHURCH, RIESEL

in," she emphasized, "we're really going to have to go to an every-Sunday situation." The few Springhill members who remained in the neighborhood of the church were older adults, and most of the younger families with children and teenagers lived ten miles away in Mart or fifteen or more miles away in Waco. They passed open and active urban churches every time they drove to Springhill, and many attended those churches on first and third Sundays, when Springhill held Sunday-school classes only. The trip to Sunday school on odd Sundays might be more worthwhile for them if worship followed. "Young people now want to be involved," explained Gibson, a challenge best met, she thought, by "trying to really convince them to see their need for the church, their need to be in the church and participate in the church as a way of acting out their faith."[24] Once the church commits to weekly services, Gibson's work will double, increasing her motivation to develop lay leadership to assume much of the extra load.

Adding additional services was a goal successfully achieved at Goshen Cumberland Presbyterian Church in America through the leadership of Pastor Roosevelt Fields, who estimated that 90 percent of his active membership lived in the city and drove to the country for church among family and longtime friends. Gradually, Fields led the church into weekly services. When the new schedule proved successful, then he began introducing the idea of holding Wednesday night prayer meeting and Bible study. He told the congregation he was going to be there every Wednesday night regardless of how many people came. The number in attendance grew from one person on the first Wednesday night to a faithful dozen within a few months. Increasing his share of the ministry from part-time to full-time had no effect on Fields's salary; it remained at the part-time level.[25]

Birome Church, down from 145 members in 1945 to nineteen in 1999, relocated a former school building next door and named it the community center. When area youth requested use of the building for dances or other recreation purposes, however, Birome members voted against the idea. William Gardiner Ellis, Birome's pastor for more than fifty years, admitted that "the rural church has not adapted itself." Providing for community needs must accompany preaching the gospel, he claimed. "A church today," he confessed, "to really attract and hold a people has got to have everything imaginable. Everything imaginable!"[26] Failure to extend its facilities to the community may have played a part in the demise of the Birome Church, which closed in 2001.

What, then, do these churches, survivors for 75 to 136 years, see as their futures? Some dedicated members of Central Texas open-country churches have firm optimism, others hope for the best, and a few do not expect the church to outlive their generation.

One measure of a congregation's stability is the physical evidence presented by the church building itself. Maintenance denotes promise for the future, while deterioration signals a fading hope. Evidence of confidence in the future of Springhill United Methodist included a plan to collect memorial funds for replacing the ten sanctuary windows with stained glass. Following its longstanding tradition of paying-as-you-go, the church did not consider using tithes and operating funds for such decorations. Memorial donations, not Sunday offerings, will furnish the new windows. Ernestine Anderson explained, "God doesn't really care whether you have stained glass or not, but it's nice to have the beauty."[27]

Members of Canaan Baptist Church also demonstrated security in their congregation's future with the recent application of exterior vinyl siding to the sanctuary. Canaan's prospects for the future brightened considerably after 1999, when B. F. Engelbrecht sold his ranch on Prairie Chapel Road to George W. Bush, then serving as Texas governor. During Bush's first two years as U.S. president, he and his family visited Canaan Baptist Church on Easter morning, drawing international attention to the century-old church on the wildflower prairie west of Crawford.[28]

In contrast to the careful maintenance employed at Springhill and Canaan churches, St. Paul's United Church of Christ, Cego, voted against making roof and foundation repairs on its seventy-five-year-old sanctuary. The congregation had declined to thirty-five members, less than a dozen of whom attended regularly. All the remaining active members were more than fifty years old. "That decision not to repair our building," stated Pastor Jeffrey Taylor, "we recognized as provisional—we could change our mind; we don't think we will—but at least a provisional decision to write our last chapter." Although the church was able financially to fund the needed repairs, Taylor explained that the members decided that it was too much money "to spend on ourselves given that we did not see ourselves as really having prospects for the future."[29]

Adding to the congregation's concern was the recent closure of their neighbor church, Cego Baptist, where Sunday-school membership fell from nineteen to seven between 1994 and 1995, the last year it had a pastor.[30] By 1997, the church on the hill above the Cego cemetery stood abandoned. A set of windows from one of its twin towers lay on the ground by the church door, a tangled vine overtook its crooked and faded sign, and only a deteriorating carpet held together the sagging floor boards. The last time someone slipped the cardboard numbers into the register board, five people had attended Sunday school.

For the few remaining members of St. Paul's, Cego, talk of disbanding is still too uncomfortable, so they hold services in the parish hall now that the sanctuary is completely unfit for services. Lifelong member Alice Miller, reflecting upon past hardships survived by the church through several generations, remarked, "Part of what I'm doing right now is thinking about there's no future in it, but you have to have faith that we'll be there another year, another two years, that we can make it. We will hold on just as long as we can." "They're talking like it's a vision for another fifty years, and we're pretty sure that can't happen," confessed Lorraine Kluge, whose husband pastored the church from 1970 to 1994. "But," she added, "it's that kind of vision and their faith that keeps them going."[31]

Members of African American rural churches view continued communication and cooperation with one another as a key to their futures. Pastors came and went within these rural congregations, but the stability of their core memberships and the extent of their shared history created strong ties. Ernestine Anderson recognized the political significance of cooperation among the rural churches, believing "divided you just can't survive." Self-initiated isolation from other like churches, Anderson believed, may have contributed to the closing of Holder's Chapel African Methodist Episcopal Church in Harrison. The church met from 1873 until the 1990s, when through death, old age, sickness, and migration, the membership had dwindled to the point where the church was no longer sustainable. Anderson remarked that in its later years the Holder's Chapel congregation "stayed within themselves in their worship services," forfeiting the support enjoyed by those churches who shared resources during lean times and thereby survived.[32]

The loss of a church like Holder's Chapel caused great concern among "the family of churches" who worried about a similar fate. When waning churches revived, sister churches received a breath of new hope. Mount Moriah Baptist Church, which anchored the eastern end of Mount Moriah Road, opposite Springhill United Methodist on the west, was once a thriving congregation that fellowshipped faithfully with area churches. As its older members died and its younger ones moved away, the church managed to meet only once a month, if at all. In 1998, a new pastor took control of Mount Moriah. A resident of Calvert, thirty miles south, the pastor began carrying vanloads of young people and children to Mount Moriah for church. On Saturdays, the vans returned from Calvert for socials. That September, the church joined with other guest churches for Springhill's

133rd annual homecoming. Ernestine Anderson recalled that Mount Moriah brought to the afternoon services at Springhill "a van and a half of young people, and most of those young people were in the choir and they were just spirit-filled, and they had such a good time that we had a good time, too." The gifts of youth and spirit provided by one church encouraged the other churches with renewed hope for their own futures.[33]

Loyalty to family and ethnic heritage, identification with the church environs and traditional values, memories of spiritual births and renewals, and flexibility in the face of change kept together many open-country congregations on the Central Texas prairie. Through the twentieth century, agrarian lifestyles evaporated and community landmarks disappeared. For a fortunate few, a house of worship still stands on the prairie, a reminder of the state's agricultural past and a symbol of steadfast Christian faith.

PHOTOGRAPHER'S NOTE

Photographers bring all of who they are to the picture-making process. As such, the resulting photographs, whether made as document or fine art, are interpretations. Although fixed firmly in reality, I hope these photographs go beyond pure documentation of the rural church to explore the spirit of the story. Each of the photographs represents, among other things, the expression of a longing to worship God, and the images serve as evidence of a desire to live within and contribute to a close community. Aesthetically, the compositions are (as many of the subjects themselves) simple and straightforward. No artifice.

The photographs were made with hand-held 35mm and medium-format cameras. The hand-held camera gives the photographer a different set of possibilities from that of the tripod-mounted camera. In particular, the hand-held encourages spontaneity.

The images were captured and printed on silver gelatin media the way the Good Lord intended. This project was envisioned in black and white from the start for more than just archival quality. Black-and-white photographs are considerably more than images without color. Working in black and white allowed me to concentrate on content, form, and tonality without the added visual complexities and sometime distractions of color. Also, black-and-white photographs are rich in detail, dignity, and sensuality.

Images need text to be fully understood and appreciated and when done well this combination of text and image becomes stronger than either element standing alone. The authors' text here has added much-needed voice, time, and significance to the photographs.

The photographs in this volume are the result of pleasurable digging in my own backyard. So often, innumerable visual treasures lie unnoticed locally as we search for the exotic faraway. Navigating the back roads close to home, so key to the completion of this work, was an unanticipated

SHADOW OF THE PHOTOGRAPHER, ST. MARTIN'S CATHOLIC CEMETERY, TOURS

joy. Additionally, I found that the more invested and knowledgeable I became about the rural church over time the more personal and expressive my photographs became. I shot a greater percentage of "keepers" later in the project than I did during the earlier stages.

—Clark G. Baker

ABBREVIATIONS FOR LOCATIONS:

IOH Institute for Oral History, Baylor University, Waco, Texas
TXC The Texas Collection, Baylor University, Waco, Texas

PREFACE

1. D. W. Meinig, *Imperial Texas: An Interpretive Essay in Cultural Geography,* 108.
2. For a description of the Blackland Prairie, see Mary Rebecca Sharpless, "Fertile Ground, Narrow Choices: Women on Cotton Farms of the Texas Blackland Prairie, 1900–1940" (Ph.D. diss., Emory University, 1993), 1–57.
3. U.S. Department of Commerce, Bureau of the Census, *Fifteenth Census of the United States,* vol. 3, part 2, *Population,* 1017.
4. Louisa Romans DuPuy, "Social Trends in McLennan County, Texas" (master's thesis, Baylor University, 1934), 90.
5. Clark Graham Baker, "Photography as Document: A Study of Family Photography and Its Viability as a Truth-Telling Medium" (Ph.D. diss., University of Alabama, 1995).
6. Meinig, *Imperial Texas,* 109.

CHAPTER 1

1. The rise and fall of agrarian communities in Central Texas between 1865 and 1930 paralleled other southern regions as described by Edward L. Ayers, *The Promise of the New South: Life after Reconstruction.*
2. Vivian Elizabeth Smyrl, "McLennan County," in *The New Handbook of Texas,* ed. Ron Tyler et al.; W. R. Poage, *McLennan County—Before 1980,* 45, 46–47; "Falls of the Brazos River," Texas Historical

Commission, *Texas Historic Sites Atlas*, available on the Internet at <http://atlas.thc.state.tx.us/> (cited hereinafter as *Texas Historic Sites Atlas*).

3. "County Population History," *Texas Almanac 1992–1993, Dallas Morning News,* 1991, 163–78.

4. Farmers from eastern Norway thought the Bosque County landscape was similar to that of their homeland. Our Savior's Lutheran Church, Norse, Texas, *Our Savior's Lutheran Church Centennial Celebration, 1869–1969,* [7].

5. Randolph B. Campbell and Richard G. Lowe, *Wealth and Power in Antebellum Texas,* 28, 141.

6. Randolph B. Campbell, *An Empire for Slavery: The Peculiar Institution in Texas, 1821–1865,* 265.

7. Inter-University Consortium for Political and Social Research, "Census Data for the Year 1860," *Historical United States Census Data Browser,* available on the Internet at <http://fisher.lib.virginia.edu/census> [accessed February 14, 2001] (cited hereinafter as *Historical U.S. Census Browser*).

8. National Archives and Records Services, Population Schedules of the Eighth Census of the United States, 1860, Schedule 2: Slave Inhabitants.

9. Poage, *McLennan County,* 55–57; Dayton Kelley, ed., *The Handbook of Waco and McLennan County, Texas,* 59–60.

10. Campbell, *Empire for Slavery,* 264–65.

11. Dickson D. Bruce, Jr., "Frontier, Influence of," in *Encyclopedia of Religion in the South,* ed. Samuel S. Hill. For a discussion of western evangelicalism, see Nathan O. Hatch, *The Democratization of American Christianity* (New Haven: Yale University Press, 1989) and Anne C. Loveland, *Southern Evangelicals and the Social Order, 1800–1860* (Baton Rouge: Louisiana State University Press, 1980).

12. Percentages are from an 1858 Methodist report of 200 members in Waco and 34 in the countryside, in Macum Phelan, *A History of Early Methodism in Texas, 1817–1866,* 426; and from 1860 Baptist reports of 181 members in Waco and 156 in country churches, in J. L. Walker and C. P. Lumpkin, *History of the Waco Baptist Association of Texas,* 27. In 1860, no more than 12 percent of Texans were affiliated with any organized religion. John W. Storey, "Religion," in *New Handbook of Texas.*

13. Norman W. Spellman, "Methodist Church," in *New Handbook of Texas.*

14. Ronald C. Ellison, *Texas and Baptist Sunday Schools, 1829–1996,* 10–11, 17. The two earliest Texas Baptist churches were at Nacogdoches and Bastrop. Hardshell Baptist influence remained primarily in East Texas. Harry Leon McBeth, *Texas Baptists: A Sesquicentennial History,* 17–18, 21–23. Morrell left an account of his travels and the founding of Baptist organizations throughout the state in *Flowers and Fruits from the Wilderness, or Forty-Six Years in Texas and Two Winters in Honduras* (Boston: Gould and Lincoln, 1872).

15. John W. Storey, "Baptist Church," in *New Handbook of Texas;* J. M. Carroll, *Texas Baptist Statistics, 1895,* 5; McBeth, *Texas Baptists,* 33–36, 41, 48–49.
16. J. M. Carroll, *A History of Texas Baptists,* ed. by J. B. Cranfill, 254.
17. Ibid., 255; McBeth, *Texas Baptists,* 53–54.
18. Walter N. Vernon et al., *The Methodist Excitement in Texas: A History,* 87–88.
19. Poage, *McLennan County,* 129; Kelley, *Handbook of Waco and McLennan County,* 187; Phelan, *Early Methodism in Texas,* 384, 426, 489.
20. Phelan, *Early Methodism in Texas,* 386, 388.
21. In 1859, Speegle helped organize Pleasant Grove Baptist Church, which years later became Speegleville Baptist Church. The church moved twice with the community, which was displaced first in 1928 and later in 1951 with the construction and later enlargement of Lake Waco dam. Speegleville became a Waco suburb. Poage, *McLennan County,* 50, 128–29, 248.
22. Kelley, *Handbook of Waco and McLennan County,* 17, 187.
23. In the 1870s and 1880s these churches moved into new railroad towns. Bold Springs merged with West; White Rock with Chalk Bluff; and Onion Springs with McGregor. See "First Baptist Church of West," "Chalk Bluff Baptist Church," and "First Baptist Church of McGregor," in *Texas Historic Sites Atlas.*
24. Notes from church minutes at Cow Bayou, which disunited after World War I, appear in Library of Congress American Memory Collection, "Mrs. Amanda E. Lockered," in *American Life Histories: Manuscripts from the Federal Writers' Project, 1936–1940,* available on the Internet at <http://memory. loc.gov/ammem/wpaintro/wpahome.html> [accessed February 19, 2001].
25. The history of Waco University is condensed in Carroll, *Texas Baptist Statistics 1895,* 15.
26. Reports from the 1850s on slave memberships in a few Texas Baptist associations are provided in Carroll, *History of Texas Baptists,* 257–60. The Waco association's lack of ministry among blacks is stated in Walker and Lumpkin, *Waco Baptist Association,* 37.
27. Richard Elam, "Baptist Ministers and Slavery in Antebellum Texas," in *Texas Baptist History* 9 (1989): 3.
28. Carroll, *History of Texas Baptists,* 335.
29. See Texas state historical marker citations for "Bosqueville Methodist Church" and "Bosqueville Baptist Church" in *Texas Historic Sites Atlas.* Vivian Elizabeth Smyrl and Mary M. Standifer, "Bosque College and Seminary," in *New Handbook of Texas.* After World War I, Bosqueville became a Waco suburb.
30. In the 1880s, Perry's church members split and joined separate, newly organized churches in the new railroad town of Moody. See "First Baptist Church of Moody" and "Moody United Methodist Church," in *Texas Historic Sites Atlas.*

31. Effects of the war on Texas churches are compiled from Carroll, *History of Texas Baptists,* 317–26; McBeth, *Texas Baptists,* 60–61; Robert A. Baker, *The Blossoming Desert: A Concise History of Texas Baptists,* 115–18; Phelan, *Early Methodism in Texas,* 463–73; and Vernon et al., *Methodist Excitement in Texas,* 120–23.

32. Sarah Joyce Rutherford Starr, "'Yours Heart and Hand': An Analysis of the Correspondence of James and Patience Crain Black, 1861–1865" (master's thesis, Baylor University, 1990), 45–46, 88–89, 103.

33. Federal troops, concentrating on the western borders, had little effect in changing the social order or controlling violence in Texas and did not reach McLennan County until 1868. With the 1873 election of Governor Richard Coke of McLennan County, white conservative "redemption" was complete in Texas, the fourth southern state to return to Democratic politics. See Ayers, *Promise of the New South,* 8; Kelley, *Handbook of Waco and McLennan County,* 221; and Carl H. Moneyhon, "Reconstruction," in *New Handbook of Texas.*

34. From 1860 to 1870, McLennan County's black population almost doubled, but the percentage of blacks among the total county population fell from 38.6 percent to 34.3 percent. *Historical U.S. Census Browser* online. On violence in Central Texas, see William Dean Carrigan, "Between South and West: Race, Violence, and Power in Central Texas, 1836–1916" (Ph.D. diss., Emory University, 1999).

35. *Texas Almanac 1992–93,* 163–78.

36. DuPuy, "Social Trends," appended map. DuPuy's map, based on courthouse records and "discussions with citizens familiar with the county" (p. 90), proved fairly accurate. Discrepancies noted below are based on personal visits to church locations and are confirmed by the 1936 Texas State Highway Department map of McLennan County, which delineated church sites.

37. Poage, *McLennan County,* 87–95, 238–70, describes railroads and their effects on area communities. Crawford, Downsville, Elm Mott, Hallsburg, Harrison, Patton, and South Bosque were older communities that benefited from the railroads. New rail towns included Axtell, Battle, Bruceville, Eddy, Hewitt, Lakeview, Leroy, Lorena, Mart, McGregor, Moody, Riesel, Ross, Tokio, and West.

38. Communities with congregations that moved included those cited above in earlier notes, plus Mastersville, which moved into Eddy; Comanche Springs, Banks, and Eagle Springs into McGregor; and White Hall and Stanford Chapel into Hewitt.

39. DuPuy, "Social Trends," appended map. DuPuy's map mislabeled the Riesel German Evangelical church as Lutheran and did not identify Meyers Memorial Methodist Church in Riesel as German.

40. DuPuy, "Social Trends," appended map. Historic open-country churches excluded from DuPuy's

map included St. Peter's Evangelical Church between Gerald and West; Olive Branch Baptist, between Axtell and Leroy; and Oak Grove Baptist, north of China Spring. DuPuy mistakenly identified the white New Hope Baptist Church near Riesel as African American and failed to indicate Willow Grove Baptist outside Speegleville was African American. The map identified the historic German Evangelical church at Gerald as Lutheran. DuPuy did not designate the ethnic affiliations of Canaan German Baptist Church west of Crawford or Meier Settlement German Methodist Church north of Riesel. The map misplaced a white Baptist church named Liberty Hill next to a black Baptist church by the same name near South Bosque. In fact, the white Liberty Hill Baptist Church was located between Eddy and Moody.

41. McLennan County, Deed Records, P: 116, Waco, Texas.

42. Renee Monroe, "The Community of South Bosque" (1977, photocopy of typescript, IOH), 3–5, 11, 13–14, 18–19; Poage, *McLennan County,* 239–40.

43. Geneva Maxwell Russell, *Oral Memoirs of Geneva Maxwell Russell,* interviewed by Lois E. Myers, on eight occasions from September 2 through November 11, 1992, in Woodway, Texas (TXC, 1998), 102–107.

44. By 1990, African Americans accounted for only 15.6 percent of the total McLennan County population. *Texas Almanac 2000–2001, Dallas Morning News,* 1999, 229.

45. Brush arbors were commonly used during summer camp meetings, but in their early years, many black churches met in brush arbors year round. Mount Olive Missionary Baptist Church, Downsville, was originally called "The Brushie" because it met in a brush arbor for its first five years. See Dickson D. Bruce, Jr., "Brush Arbor," in *Encyclopedia of Religion in the South;* and Souvenir Booklet Committee, *Mt. Olive Missionary Baptist Church, Downsville, Texas: 100th Year Anniversary, 1884–1984* (n.p., 1984, TXC), 6. On community use of rural churches, see William E. Montgomery, "The Formation of African American Churches," in Clyde McQueen, *Black Churches in Texas: A Guide to Historic Congregations,* 14–15.

46. Baptist associations and conventions were voluntary, fluid organizations that divided and subdivided over the years. Generally, historic African American Baptist churches in Central Texas aligned with the Good Hope Western District Missionary Baptist Association (since 1870), the Willow Grove Baptist Association (since 1880), and the Union Baptist Association (since 1896). Garry H. Radford, Sr., *African American Heritage in Waco, Texas,* 61–62.

47. William E. Montgomery, *Under Their Own Vine and Fig Tree: The African-American Church in the South, 1865–1900,* 105.

48. McLennan County, Deed Records, T: 372–73.

49. "Downsville: 'It's home, and to me it's the prettiest place in the world,'" *Waco Tribune-Herald,* December 18, 1987, 9A.

50. McLennan County, Deed Records, 54: 37.

51. McLennan County, Deed Records, 93: 198–99. Mount Olive Missionary Baptist Church moved into Downsville in 1980. The church experienced stability in leadership, having only eleven pastors in its first one hundred years. Souvenir Booklet Committee, *Mt. Olive Missionary Baptist Church,* 6–8.

52. Kay Barrett, "Willow Grove history rich success tale," *Waco Tribune-Herald,* July 27, 1997; McLennan County, Deed Records, 332: 621–22.

53. Mount Zion CME Church, organized in Waco in 1901, is reportedly the only CME congregation in McLennan County. Radford, *African American Heritage in Waco,* 34.

54. I. B. Loud, "Methodism and the Negroes," in Olin W. Nail, ed., *History of Texas Methodism 1900–1960,* 97. In 1939, after ninety-five years of separation, the northern and southern divisions of the Methodist Episcopal Church reunited. The Central Jurisdiction was formed for the nation's black Methodist Episcopal churches, and the West Texas Conference continued to operate under its authority until the 1960 merger of several Methodist bodies into the United Methodist Church and the subsequent integration of conferences. For a discussion of the separation of the races within United Methodism, see William B. McClain, *Black People in the Methodist Church: Whither Thou Goest?* (Cambridge, Mass.: Schenkman Publishing Company, 1984), 90–99.

55. McLennan County, Deed Records, 21: 483; Ernestine Garrett Anderson, tape-recorded interviews by Lois E. Myers, February 17 and March 30, 1999, in Riesel, Texas (IOH, 1999, transcript); "A New Church for a New World: Official Opening of Spring Hill United Methodist Church, Riesel, Texas, February 23, 1969" (n.p., 1969, photocopy, IOH), n.p.

56. Douglas Hales, "Paul Quinn College," in *New Handbook of Texas;* McLennan County, Deed Records, 75:40; Jay M. Butler, "James Harrison and the Development of Harrison Switch" (master's thesis, Baylor University, 1989), 75, 82.

57. Thomas H. Campbell, *History of the Cumberland Presbyterian Church in Texas,* 12.

58. Gene A. Barnett, "William K. Sadler Family," in Bosque County History Book Committee, *Bosque County: Land and People,* vol. 1, 649. Cumberland Presbyterians commonly accepted slave members, according to Thomas H. Campbell, *Good News on the Frontier: A History of the Cumberland Presbyterian Church,* 73–74. In 1874, the Cumberland Presbyterian Church, Colored, separated from the white church. In 1960, the denomination became the Second Cumberland Presbyterian Church, and in 1992, the Cumberland Presbyterian Church in America.

59. R. Douglas Brackenridge, *Voice in the Wilderness: A History of the Cumberland Presbyterian Church in Texas,* 92.

60. Rock Springs, near Valley Mills, was the center of an all-black community known as The Colony, described in Bertha Sadler, *Portrait of a Pioneer in the Making, James B. Sadler, 1828–1911,* 5–7; and Samuel Adams, "Members gather to commemorate 100th anniversary of church," *Waco Tribune-Herald,* November 5, 1990, 3C.

61. McLennan County, Probate Records, 2040; Deed Records, 471: 347.

62. Jay P. Dolan, "The Immigrants and Their Gods: A New Perspective in American Religious History," in Henry Warner Bowden and P. C. Kemeny, eds., *American Church History: A Reader,* 65.

63. Our Savior's Lutheran Church, *Centennial Celebration,* [7–13]; Pierson, "Norwegian Settlements in Bosque County, Texas" (master's thesis, University of Texas, 1947), 87, 90–92.

64. Fifteenth Census of the United States, vol. 3, part 2, *Population,* 1017, 1021.

65. The majority of Catholic parishes in rural areas in the nation were German, according to John L. Shover, *First Majority, Last Minority: The Transforming of Rural Life in America,* 43.

66. Mary Dvoracek, *Church of the Assumption, West, Texas, Centennial, 1892–1992* (West, Tex.: Czechoslovak Publishing Company, 1992, TXC), 15; Mary Elizabeth Jupe, *A History of Tours, Texas,* v, 5, 8, 106; Poage, *McLennan County,* 262.

67. Dvoracek, *Church of the Assumption,* 16; Jupe, *A History of Tours,* 9; Poage, *McLennan County,* 257–59. Texas attracted the largest rural Czech population in the U.S., and Czechs commonly settled among Germans and shared a Catholic parish with them. Terry Jordan et al., *Texas: A Geography,* 86.

68. Robert Cunningham, Sr., *A History of the Elk Community, Texas* (n.p., 1996, TXC), 61–62; V. A. Svrcek, trans. and ed., *Czech-Moravian Catholic Communities of Texas,* 62; *St. Joseph's Church, Elk, Texas, Dedicated December 17, 1972* (n.p., 1972), [5–10].

69. Perry United Methodist Church, *A Century of Methodism: Centennial Celebration June 25–July 2, 1972* (Perry, Tex.: Perry United Methodist Church, 1972). Methodists recruited actively among German-speaking Texans. See Vernon et al., *Methodist Excitement in Texas,* 193–95.

70. The history of the Lutheran Church-Missouri Synod in Texas began with the migration of Wends from Prussia and Saxony. See Sylvia Ann Grider, *The Wends in Texas* (San Antonio: The University of Texas Institute of Texan Cultures, 1982). Trinklein's personal memoir of the founding of Trinity Lutheran Church appears in Dorothy Kuehl and Karen Meyer, *Friedens Au: A Centennial History of Trinity Lutheran Church, Riesel, Texas* (Riesel: Trinity Lutheran Church Evening Guild, 1983, TXC), 7–17.

71. Kuehl and Meyer, *Friedens Au,* 43–44, 75; Robert J. Koenig, *Pause to Ponder: A History of the Lutheran Church-Missouri Synod of Texas* (n.p.: Texas District, The Lutheran Church-Missouri Synod, 1980), 64, 213. No Lutheran churches survived in open-country McLennan County. Two Evangelical Lutheran Church in America congregations persisted in rural Coryell County, at Coryell City and Mound.

72. Freidrich Werning's 1913 memoir, "The History of the Texas District of the German Evangelical Synod of North America," appears in Erna C. Schack, *Zion United Church of Christ 100th Anniversary, 1981–1981* (n.p., 1981, TXC), [8–11]; David Dunn et al., *A History of the Evangelical and Reformed Church*, 240–41.

73. Dates and locations of churches provided in United Church of Christ, *Year Book of the United Church of Christ*, 276–79. Dunn et al., *A History of the Evangelical and Reformed Church*, 279–95, describe the union of the two denominations.

74. The story of Baptist work among Germans appears in Carroll, *Texas Baptists*, 589–94; Lloyd Harsch, "Baptist Witness Among Germans in Texas," in *Texas Baptist History* 17 (1997): 89–123; and Albert Ray Niederer, "Baptist Missionary Activity among the German People in Texas, 1850–1950" (master's thesis, Baylor University, 1976).

75. By 1945, Cottonwood and Bethel Heights churches dropped their German Baptist affiliation in favor of the Baptist General Convention of Texas. Harsch, "Baptist Witness among Germans in Texas," 101–102, 121.

76. McLennan County, Deed Records, 99: 536; "Canaan Baptist Church, Crawford, Texas, 100th Anniversary, 1891–1991" (n.p., 1991, photocopy, IOH), n.p.; Shari Kimbrough, "Prairie Chapel Rich in History," *McGregor Mirror*, July 7, 1977, 4; and O. K. Ringering and Mrs. O. K. Ringering, *Canaan Baptist Church, Crawford, Texas, 75th Anniversary, Seventy-Five Years, 1891–1966* (n.p., 1966, TXC), n.p.

77. Lawrence A. Cardoso, *Mexican Emigration to the United States 1897–1931: Socio-Economic Patterns*, 2, 5–7.

78. Carey McWilliams, *North from Mexico: The Spanish-Speaking People of the United States*, 169–70.

79. Marla Pierson, "Preserving a church's legacy," *Waco Tribune-Herald*, April 29, 2000, 10A; Carlos E. Castañeda, *The Church in Texas since Independence, 1836–1950*, vol. 7, *Our Catholic Heritage in Texas*, 245–46. The history of the Waco Mexican mission is given in *Souvenir of the Dedication of St. Francis Church, on Thanksgiving Day, November 26, 1931* (n.p., 1931, TXC), 25–31.

80. *Texas Almanac 1992–1993*, 166, 178. McLennan County urbanization came earlier than average in Texas, where statewide, urban populations outstripped rural ones during the 1940s. See Terry G. Jordan et al., *Texas: A Geography*, 49.

81. Under the crop-lien system, a tenant farmer, furnishing his own tools and work stock, paid part of his crop—normally a third of the corn and a fourth of the cotton—in return for the use of the owner's land and sometimes a year's worth of supplies. A sharecropper, who furnished only his own labor and that of his family and depended on the landlord to supply everything from seed to mules, split the crop down the middle with the owner. Other landless farm laborers worked for minimal

wages, usually on a seasonal basis. Effects of the crop-lien system on families and churches are provided in Rebecca Sharpless, *Fertile Land, Narrow Choices: Women on Texas Cotton Farms, 1900–1940,* 7–12, 204, 205.

82. Michael Berger, *The Devil Wagon in God's Country: The Automobile and Social Change in Rural America, 1893–1929,* 51, 212.

83. "Highway Development," in *New Handbook of Texas;* Poage, *McLennan County,* 104.

84. Una Bedichek and George T. Baskett, *The Consolidation of Rural Schools with and without Transportation,* Bulletin of the University of Texas no. 43, General Series no. 7 (Austin: University of Texas, 1904), 4; William E. Cantrell, "Some Advantages of School Consolidation in Bosque, Coryell, Hill, Lampasas, and McLennan Counties" (master's thesis, Southern Methodist University, 1931), 15, 32, 38; DuPuy, "Social Trends," 77–78.

85. On the factors leading to the closing of general stores, see Thomas J. Schlereth, *Victorian America: Transformations in Everyday Life, 1876–1915,* 143–46; and Thomas D. Clark, *Pills, Petticoats, and Plows: The Southern Country Store,* xiii.

86. Gilbert Fite, *Cotton Fields No More: Southern Agriculture 1865–1980,* 169–70; Poage, *McLennan County,* 117.

87. *Texas Almanac 1992–1993,* 166, 178.

88. Kristi Strickland, "Bosque County"; Lisa C. Maxwell, "Falls County"; and Vivian Elizabeth Smyrl, "Coryell County," in *New Handbook of Texas.*

89. Spring Valley Methodist survives in the city of Hewitt.

90. Rachel M. Marley and Evelyn Riggs Posey, *Gone but Not Forgotten: A History of Battle Cemetery and Battle Community,* 371–74, 377, 381, 385–89.

91. Monroe, "South Bosque," 13–14, 20, 22–23; "Harris Creek Baptist Church," in *Texas Historic Sites Atlas.*

92. *Annual of the Baptist General Convention of Texas* (Dallas: Baptist General Convention of Texas, 1990, 1999).

93. U.S. Department of Agriculture, U.S. National Agricultural Statistics Service, "Table 2: Number of Farms 1997 and 1992," available online from *1997 Census of Agriculture,* <http://www.nass.usda.gov/census > [accessed February 22, 2001].

94. Changes in Texas agriculture are recorded in *Texas Almanac 2000–2001,* 565–66.

CHAPTER 2

1. Donald Richter and Wilma Richter, tape-recorded interview by Lois E. Myers, September 8, 1998, in Leroy, Texas (IOH, 1998, transcript); Alice Margaret Miller, tape-recorded interview by Lois E. Myers, January 22, 1999, in Marlin, Texas (IOH, 1999, transcript).

2. Oris Pierson, *Oral Memoirs of Oris Pierson,* interviewed by Suzanne Olsen, November 2 and 29, 1972, in Clifton, Texas (TXC, 1974), 64; Benjamin Franklin Engelbrecht, *Oral Memoirs of Canaan Baptist Church,* interviewed by Rebecca Sharpless, on February 13, 1997, and (with Earlien Freyer Engelbrecht) on March 25, April 2, and April 22, 1997, in Crawford, Texas (TXC, 2002), 146.

3. Eunice Brown Johnson, *Oral Memoirs of Eunice Brown Johnson,* interviewed by Rebecca Sharpless, July 31, 1986, in Gatesville, Texas (TXC, 2000), 12.

4. Ima Hoppe Bekkelund, *Oral Memoirs of Canaan Baptist Church,* interviewed by Lois E. Myers, February 25, 1997, in Woodway, Texas (TXC, 2002), 14–15, 33.

5. Glenda Gala Garrett, tape-recorded interview by Lois E. Myers, June 22, 1998, in Waco, Texas (IOH, 1998, transcript).

6. Evelyn Bohne and Louise Yows, tape-recorded interview by Marla Pierson Lester, February 7, 2001, in Coryell City (IOH, 2001, transcript); Robert Carl Scott, *Oral Memoirs of Canaan Baptist Church,* interviewed by Rebecca Sharpless, May 15, 1997, in Waco, Texas (TXC, 2002), 473; Lorraine Kaufman Kluge, tape-recorded interview by Lois E. Myers, January 13, 1999, in Waco, Texas (IOH, 1999, transcript).

7. Carol Grant Gibson, tape-recorded interview by Lois E. Myers, June 22, 1998, in Waco, Texas (IOH, 1998, transcript); Anderson, interview, March 30, 1999. Memorial gifts from 1978 through 1998 are listed in "Springhill United Methodist Church, Riesel, Texas, 133rd Annual Homecoming Services, September 10, 11, 13, 1998" (n.p., 1998, IOH), n.p.

8. Isidore Rozychi, tape-recorded interview by Lois E. Myers, June 3, 1998, in Tours, Texas (IOH, 1998, transcript).

9. "Flames Damage Gerald Church," *Waco Tribune-Herald,* February 9, 1978; Albert Henry Leuschner, tape-recorded interview by Lois E. Myers, February 9, 1998, in Waco, Texas (IOH, 1998, transcript); "75th Anniversary Celebration, October 25–26, 1975, St. Paul's United Church of Christ, Gerald, 1900–1975" (n.p., 1975, photocopy, IOH).

10. William Gardiner Ellis, tape-recorded interview by Lois E. Myers, January 27, 2000, in Waco, Texas (IOH, 2000, transcript); Margaret H. Norman Smith and Garnet Leon Vardeman, tape-recorded interview by Lois E. Myers, June 14, 2000, in Hewitt, Texas (IOH, 2000, transcript).

11. Smith and Vardeman, interview, June 14, 2000; A. Miller, interview, January 22, 1999; Corine Niesen

Miller, tape-recorded interview by Lois E. Myers, February 22, 1999, in Waco, Texas (IOH, 1999, transcript); Walter Dulock, Evelyn Mae Smajstrla Cunningham, Robert Cunningham, and Rosalee Smajstrla Urbis, tape-recorded interview by Lois E. Myers, September 15, 1998, in Elk, Texas (IOH, 1998, transcript).

12. Garrett, interview, June 22, 1998.

13. Mary Hanak Simcik, *Oral Memoirs of Mary Hanak Simcik,* interviewed by LaWanda Ball, November 24, 1975, in Waco, Texas (TXC, 1977), 35–36.

14. Bessie Lee Barrens Stafford, *Oral Memoirs of Bessie Lee Barrens Stafford,* interviewed by Rebecca Sharpless, May 7, 1987, in Waco, Texas (TXC, 2000), 8; Rowena Weatherly Keatts, *Oral Memoirs of Rowena Weatherly Keatts,* interviewed by Rebecca Sharpless, on five occasions from May 5, 1986, to April 15, 1987, in Waco, Texas (TXC, 2000), 150.

15. Anderson, interviews, February 17 and March 30, 1999; Garrett, interview, June 22, 1998.

16. A. Miller, interview, January 22, 1999.

17. Jerry Gauer, *Oral Memoirs of Canaan Baptist Church,* interviewed by Lois E. Myers, January 9, 1998, in Crawford, Texas (TXC, 2002), 212–13, 236; Van Doren Massirer, *Oral Memoirs of Canaan Baptist Church,* interviewed by Lois E. Myers, January 9, 1998, in Crawford, Texas (TXC, 2002), 417–18.

18. Pierson, *Oral Memoirs,* 30–31, 39.

19. V. Massirer, *Oral Memoirs,* 365–66.

20. Robert Schiemenz, *The First Hundred Years: A History of St. Paul's United Church of Christ, Gerald, Texas,* 19–20.

21. Kluge, interview, January 13, 1999; Lorraine Kluge, "History of St. Paul U.C.C." (1999, typescript, IOH); Jeffrey W. Taylor, tape-recorded interview by Lois E. Myers, February 25, 1999, in Waco, Texas (IOH, 1999, transcript); Lorene Wittner, tape-recorded interviews by Glenn Jonas, June 19, 1990, and February 6, 1991, in Cego, Texas (IOH, 1991, transcript).

22. B. Engelbrecht, with E. Engelbrecht, *Oral Memoirs,* 166–67, 169; Bekkelund, *Oral Memoirs,* 26–27.

23. B. Engelbrecht, with E. Engelbrecht, *Oral Memoirs,* 169–70, 173; Bekkelund, *Oral Memoirs,* 26–27.

24. Edna Jaeckle Dreyer, *Oral Memoirs of Canaan Baptist Church,* interviewed by Lois E. Myers, May 21, 1997, in Gatesville, Texas (TXC, 2002), 39, 44, 46–47.

25. B. Engelbrecht, with E. Engelbrecht, *Oral Memoirs,* 60, 73–74, 87–88, 97; Henry T. Engelbrecht, *Oral Memoirs of Henry T. Engelbrecht,* interviewed by Ray Niederer, March 21, 1973, in Crawford, Texas (TXC, 1974), 49, 55.

26. Dulock, E. Cunningham, R. Cunningham, and Urbis, interview, September 15, 1998; Rozychi, interview, June 3, 1998.

27. Simcik, *Oral Memoirs,* 37–38. The Czech Protestants claimed roots dating to 1415 and the work of

religious reformer John Hus. Following centuries of persecution in Europe, many Czech Protestants migrated to Texas and organized churches. In 1903, they formed a denomination called Unity of the Brethren in Texas. In the early twenty-first century, twenty-seven churches composed the denomination. The congregations appeared in both urban and rural settings. Brethren members in McLennan County worshipped at West. In adjacent Bell County, rural Brethren churches survived at Ocker and Seaton. "A Historical Sketch" and "Congregations" at *Unity of the Brethren,* available on the Internet at <http://www.unityofthebrethren.org> [accessed August 1, 2002].

28. Robert Chavez, tape-recorded interview by Marla Pierson Lester, February 1, 2001, in Waco, Texas (IOH, 2001, transcript). The significance of Our Lady of Guadalupe as the symbol of Mexican nationalism, particularly among the poor, is discussed in Jay P. Dolan and Gilberto Hinojosa, eds., *Mexican Americans and the Catholic Church, 1900–1965* (Notre Dame, Ind.: University of Notre Dame Press, 1994), 92–93, 110, 121, 181.

29. Martin Vasquez, tape-recorded interview by Marla Pierson Lester, February 6, 2001, in Waco, Texas (IOH, 2001, transcript).

30. Using shared church services among various black denominations in the rural South as an illustration, Bruce T. Grindal stated, "The character of black religiosity transcends specific church affiliation," in "The Religious Interpretation of Experience in a Black Community," in *Holding on to the Land and the Lord: Kinship, Ritual, Land Tenure, and Social Policy in the Rural South,* ed. Robert L. Hall and Carol B. Stack, 92.

31. Roosevelt Fields, tape-recorded interview by Lois E. Myers, May 14, 1999, in Harrison, Texas (IOH, 1999, transcript).

32. Valerie London Willis, tape-recorded interview by Anne Radford Phillips, April 8, 1992, in Waco, Texas (IOH, 1992, transcript).

33. Cedell Evans and Rosena Evans, tape-recorded interview by Jay Butler, August 16, 1993, in Post Oak community, McLennan County, Texas (IOH, 1993, transcript).

34. Anderson, interview, March 30, 1999.

35. Barbara Hamilton Williams, tape-recorded interview by Lois E. Myers, April 21, 1998, in Waco, Texas (IOH, 1998, transcript).

CHAPTER 3

1. Rural churches fit precisely into John Brinkerhoff Jackson's description of sense of place: "a lively awareness of the familiar environment, a ritual repetition, a sense of fellowship based on a shared experience," in *A Sense of Place, A Sense of Time,* 159.

2. Anderson, interview, March 30, 1999.

3. Lawrence G. Felice, tape-recorded interview by Lois E. Myers, February 25, 1999, in Waco, Texas (IOH, 1999, transcript); "A Brief History, St. Paul United Church of Christ, Marlin, Texas" (n.p., n.d., photocopy, IOH).

4. Norma Hinze Herrington, tape-recorded interview by Glenn Jonas, June 23, 1990, in Cego, Texas (IOH, 1990, transcript); Edith Bridger McKee, tape-recorded interview by Glenn Jonas, June 21, 1990, in Cego, Texas (IOH, 1990, transcript); Dreyer, *Oral Memoirs,* 51; Bekkelund, *Oral Memoirs,* 20–21.

5. A. Leuschner, interview, February 9, 1998.

6. Lonnie Graves, tape-recorded interview by Jay Butler, June 30, 1993, in Satin, Texas (IOH, 1993, transcript).

7. Vera Estelle Allen Malone, *Oral Memoirs of Vera Malone,* interviewed by LaWanda Ball, December 5, 1975, in Waco, Texas (TXC, 1977), 9–10; Garrett, interview, June 22, 1998; Fields, interview, May 14, 1999.

8. In the late 1950s, Liberty Hill demolished its tabernacle and replaced it with a building with Sunday-school space, a dining hall, and kitchen. See Wanda Coulter Duty, tape-recorded interview by Lois E. Myers, August 11, 1998, in Eddy, Texas (IOH, 1998, transcript); Bernice Porter Bostick Weir, *Oral Memoirs of Bernice Porter Bostick Weir,* interviewed by Rebecca Sharpless, on four occasions from July 9 to August 6, 1990, in Liberty Hill community, McLennan County, Texas (TXC, 1999), 93, 124; and Gracie Johnson Rowe, tape-recorded interview by Lois E. Myers, July 7, 1998, in Eddy, Texas (IOH, 1998, transcript).

9. Schiemenz, *The First Hundred Years: St. Paul's, Gerald,* 70–71.

10. "Canaan Baptist Church, 100th Anniversary"; B. Engelbrecht, with E. Engelbrecht, *Oral Memoirs,* 59, 74–75.

11. B. Engelbrecht, with E. Engelbrecht, *Oral Memoirs,* 151–53.

12. Anderson, interview, February 17, 1999; "Springhill United Methodist Church, 133rd Homecoming."

13. Duty, interview, August 11, 1998; Wittner, interview, June 19, 1990; Dulock, E. Cunningham, R. Cunningham, and Urbis, interview, September 15, 1998.

14. Leo Simmons, tape-recorded interview by Marla Pierson Lester, February 15, 2001, in Waco, Texas (IOH, 2001, tape); Edna Long, tape-recorded interview by Marla Pierson Lester, February 6, 2001, in Harrison, Texas (IOH, 2001, tape).

15. Williams, interview, April 21, 1998.

16. Russell, *Oral Memoirs,* 118.

17. Agnes Gohlke Massirer, *Oral Memoirs of Canaan Baptist Church,* interviewed by Lois E. Myers, April 11, 1997 (TXC, 2002), 327–28.

18. Albert Huber and Flora Hildegard Hinze Huber, tape-recorded interview by Lois E. Myers, January 20, 1999, in Belfalls, Texas (IOH, 1999, transcript).

19. Russell, *Oral Memoirs,* 118; Dulock, E. Cunningham, R. Cunningham, and Urbis, interview, September 15, 1998; Joe Trotter, tape-recorded interview by Jay Butler, June 3, 1993, in Satin, Texas (IOH, 1993, transcript).

20. Dora Mae Hardcastle Miller, tape-recorded interview by Glenn Jonas, June 28, 1990, in Cego, Texas (IOH, 1990, transcript).

21. Minnie Weber Gauer, *Oral Memoirs of Canaan Baptist Church,* interviewed by Lois E. Myers, February 12, 1997, in Crawford, Texas (TXC, 2002), 256; Bekkelund, *Oral Memoirs,* 27.

22. Simcik, *Oral Memoirs,* 20–21.

23. Pierson, *Oral Memoirs,* 49.

24. Anderson, interview, February 17, 1999.

25. Lonnie Graves, tape-recorded interview by Anne Radford Phillips, October 10, 1991, in Satin, Texas (IOH, 1991, transcript).

26. Anderson, interview, March 30, 1999.

27. See Robert Michael Franklin, "The Safest Place on Earth: The Culture of Black Congregations," in *American Congregations,* vol. 2 of *New Perspectives in the Study of Congregations,* ed. James P. Wind and James W. Lewis (Chicago: University of Chicago Press, 1994), 257–60.

28. Lonnie Graves, "Cedar Grove Baptist Church" (1986, photocopy of typescript, IOH), 1, 5.

29. The appeal of churches to rural women is discussed in Sally McMillen, "No Easy Time: Rural Southern Women," in *The Rural South since World War II,* ed. R. Douglas Hurt (Baton Rouge: Louisiana State University Press, 1998), 78–79. The dominance of women in memberships of African American rural churches is presented in Hans A. Baer and Merrill Singer, *African-American Religion in the Twentieth Century: Varieties of Protest and Accommodation* (Knoxville: The University of Tennessee Press, 1992), 33.

30. Williams, interview, April 21, 1998; Gibson, interview, February 11, 1998; Garrett, interview, June 22, 1998.

31. Gibson, interview, February 11, 1998.

32. Dulock, E. Cunningham, R. Cunningham, and Urbis, interview, September 15, 1998.

33. Women's work in United Churches of Christ is described in Huber and Huber, interview, January 20, 1999; Helen Janet Miller, tape-recorded interview, by Lois E. Myers, January 26, 1999, in Waco,

Texas (IOH, 1999, transcript); A. Miller, interview, January 22, 1999; Richter and Richter, interview, September 8, 1998; Janet Terry Silaff, tape-recorded interview by Lois E. Myers, June 10, 1998, in Leroy, Texas (IOH, 1998, transcript); and in Schiemenz, *The First Hundred Years: St. Paul's, Gerald,* 78.

34. Canaan's women's missions group is discussed in Dreyer, *Oral Memoirs,* 45, 52; B. Engelbrecht, with E. Engelbrecht, *Oral Memoirs,* 148–51; H. Engelbrecht, *Oral Memoirs,* 64–65; M. Gauer, *Oral Memoirs,* 272–73; Scott, *Oral Memoirs,* 474; "Canaan Baptist Church, 100th Anniversary"; and "Southern Association Newsletter, February 2000" (Southern Association of the North American Baptist Conference, 2000, IOH).

35. Duty, interview, August 11, 1998. Examples of church benevolent acts from Anderson, interview, February 17, 1999; Rowe, interview, July 7, 1998; and John D. Hogan and Lynn Holt, tape-recorded interview by Lois E. Myers, May 30, 1998, Liberty Hill community, McLennan County, Texas (IOH, 1998, transcript).

36. John Hayden, tape-recorded interview by Lois E. Myers, December 10, 1998, in Riesel, Texas (IOH, 1998, transcript).

CHAPTER 4

1. Garrett, interview, June 22, 1998.
2. Russell, *Oral Memoirs,* 47, 101, 102–103, 104–105; Mary Ellen Nix Bullock, tape-recorded interview, by Lois E. Myers, February 15, 1996 (IOH, 1996, transcript).
3. Thomas Herrington and Dorothy Herrington, tape-recorded interview by Glenn Jonas, June 27, 1990, in Cego, Texas (IOH, 1990, transcript); McKee, interview, June 21, 1990; Wittner, interview, June 19, 1990.
4. D. Miller, interview, June 28, 1990; Wittner, interview, June 19, 1990.
5. H. Engelbrecht, *Oral Memoirs,* 26; Dreyer, *Oral Memoirs,* 44; Marvin Engelbrecht, *Oral Memoirs of Canaan Baptist Church,* interviewed by Jaclyn L. Jeffrey on March 11, 1997, in Crawford, Texas (TXC, 2002), 193–94.
6. Carl Neal, *Oral Memoirs of Carl Neal,* interviewed by Lois E. Myers on February 4 and 11, 1993, in Lorena, Texas (TXC, 1995), 48, 49; Fields, interview, May 14, 1999.
7. Charles Williams discusses the mourner's bench experience as an initiation rite in "The Conversion Ritual in a Rural Black Baptist Church," in *Holding on to the Land and the Lord,* ed. Hall and Stack, 69–79; Fields, interview, May 14, 1999.
8. Williams, interview, April 21, 1998; Anderson, interview, March 30, 1999; Garrett, interview, June 22, 1998.

9. Felice, interview, February 25, 1999.

10. Hattie Lehmann Leuschner, tape-recorded interview by Lois E. Myers, February 9, 1998, in Waco, Texas (IOH, 1998, transcript); Jane Lovett, tape-recorded interview by Lois E. Myers, February 12, 1998, in Woodway, Texas (IOH, 1998, transcript); Herman H. Blankenstein, tape-recorded interview by Lois E. Myers, April 15, 1998, in Waco, Texas (IOH, 1998, transcript); Irene Otto Blankenstein, tape-recorded interview by Lois E. Myers, April 15, 1998, in Waco, Texas (IOH, 1998, transcript); A. Leuschner, interview, February 9, 1998; Silaff, interview, June 10, 1998.

11. Dulock, E. Cunningham, R. Cunningham, and Urbis, interview, September 15, 1998.

12. A. Leuschner, interview, February 9, 1998; Richter and Richter, interview, September 8, 1998.

13. A. A. Miller, *Evangelical Church, Cego, Texas, Sunday School Minutes, Recorded by A. A. Miller, Secretary* (1941, photocopy, TXC); Huber and Huber interview, January 20, 1999. Sunday school at St. Paul's, Cego, ceased meeting by the mid 1980s.

14. H. Miller, interview, January 26, 1999.

15. Anderson, interview, March 30, 1999.

16. Wittner, interview, June 19, 1990; D. Miller, interview, June 28, 1990; T. Herrington and D. Herrington, interview, June 27, 1990; N. Herrington, interview, June 23, 1990.

17. Bohne and Yows, interview, February 7, 2001.

18. Ellis, interview, January 27, 2000.

19. Weir, *Oral Memoirs,* 116; Duty, interview, August 11, 1998.

20. Wittner, interview, June 19, 1990; McKee, interview, June 21, 1990.

21. Weir, *Oral Memoirs,* 123; Charles Brinkmeyer, tape-recorded interview by Marla Pierson Lester, February 7, 2001, in Coryell City, Texas (IOH, 2001, tape).

22. Hogan and Holt, interview, May 30, 1998.

23. Fields, interview, May 14, 1999; Felice, interview, February 25, 1999.

24. A. Leuschner, interview, February 9, 1998.

25. Lovett, interview, February 12, 1998; Liz Smiley, "Reverend Jane Lovett," in Schiemenz, *The First Hundred Years: St. Paul's, Gerald,* 13.

26. Gibson, interview, February 11, 1998; Anderson, interview, March 30, 1999.

27. Rozychi, interview, June 3, 1998; Dulock, E. Cunningham, R. Cunningham, and Urbis, interview, September 15, 1998.

28. Fred Douglas Tucker, tape-recorded interview by Jay Butler, August 26, 1993, in Falls County, Texas (IOH, 1993, transcript).

29. Pierson, *Oral Memoirs,* 64; T. Herrington and D. Herrington, interview, June 27, 1990; D. Miller,

interview, June 28, 1990; McKee, interview, June 21, 1990; Dulock, E. Cunningham, R. Cunningham, and Urbis, interview, September 15, 1998.

30. Graves, interview, June 30, 1993; Katherine Guy, tape-recorded interview by Jay Butler, July 28, 1993, in Satin, Texas (IOH, 1993, transcript).

31. B. Engelbrecht, with E. Engelbrecht, *Oral Memoirs,* 73, 78; M. Engelbrecht, *Oral Memoirs,* 207; H. Engelbrecht, *Oral Memoirs,* 75.

32. Anderson, interviews, February 17 and March 30, 1999.

33. Hogan and Holt, interview, May 30, 1998; Fields, interview, May 14, 1999.

CHAPTER 5

1. Lovett, interview, February 12, 1998; A. Leuschner, interview, February 9, 1998.

2. Bohne and Yows, interview, February 7, 2001; Brinkmeyer, interview, February 7, 2001.

3. A. Leuschner, interview, February 9, 1998; Lovett, interview, February 12, 1998; Richter and Richter, interview, September 8, 1998.

4. Gibson, interview, February 11, 1999; Anderson, interview, March 30, 1999.

5. Felice, interview, February 25, 1999; Taylor, interview, February 25, 1999. Membership data from United Church of Christ, "Find a Congregation," available online from *United Church of Christ* at <http://www.ucc.org/find/index.html> [accessed January 18, 1999].

6. C. Miller, interview, February 22, 1999; A. Miller, interview, January 22, 1999; H. Miller, interview, January 26, 1999.

7. Hogan and Holt, interview, May 30, 1998.

8. Alfred Gallmeier, tape-recorded interview by Marla Pierson, December 4, 2000, in Riesel, Texas (IOH, 2000, transcript); Kuehl and Meyer, *Friedens Au,* 30, 50.

9. Dulock, E. Cunningham, R. Cunningham, and Urbis, interview, September 15, 1998.

10. Anderson, interview, March 30, 1999; Garrett, interview, June 22, 1998.

11. Ken Camp, "Keith combats rural pastors' isolation," *Baptist Standard,* March 11, 1998, 2, 7; Liberty Hill Baptist Church Record of Progress Committee, "Record of Progress" (1966, typescript, located at Liberty Hill Baptist Church, Eddy, Texas); Hogan and Holt, interview, May 30, 1998; "Southern Baptists of Texas lists 'affiliated' churches," *Baptist Standard,* April 30, 2001, 6.

12. Kluge, interview, January 7, 1999; Huber and Huber, interview, January 20, 1999; Hayden, interview, December 10, 1998.

13. Hayden, interview, December 10, 1998. Carl S. Dudley describes the ethnic nature of the former

E&R churches within the United Church of Christ in *Where Have All Our People Gone? New Choices for Old Churches,* 102–103.

14. Kluge, interviews, January 7 and 13, 1999; Hayden, interview, December 10, 1999; Alton H. Schwecke, tape-recorded interview by Lois E. Myers, December 9, 1998, in Riesel, Texas (IOH, 1998, transcript).

15. "Momentum Gathers for New Evangelical Association," Biblical Witness Fellowship, *Biblical Witness Fellowship: Renewing the United Church of Christ,* available on the Internet at <http://www.biblical witness.org/evangelicals.html> [accessed August 5, 2002].

16. Hayden, interview, December 10, 1998; Kluge, interview, January 13, 1999.

17. Schwecke, interview, December 9, 1998; Kluge, "History of St. Paul U.C.C."; Huber and Huber, interview, January 20, 1999.

18. For NABC data, see regional summary tables of southern states in Bradley et al., *Churches and Church Membership in the United States 1990,* 7–9; and the table of Texas German Baptist churches, in Harsch, "Baptist Witness among Germans in Texas," 119–23. Scott, *Oral Memoirs,* 475; J. Gauer, *Oral Memoirs,* 215–16.

19. Anderson, interview, March 30, 1999.

20. Gibson, interview, February 11, 1999; Dulock, E. Cunningham, R. Cunningham, and Urbis, interview, September 15, 1998; Hayden, interview, December 10, 1998.

21. Gibson, interview, February 11, 1999; Anderson, interview, March 30, 1999.

22. N. Herrington, interview, June 23, 1990.

23. Hayden, interview, December 10, 1998.

24. Gibson, interview, February 11, 1999.

25. Fields, interview, May 14, 1999.

26. Ellis, interview, January 27, 2000.

27. Anderson, interview, March 30, 1999.

28. Rodney Carmichael, "A 'secret service' at sunrise," *Waco Tribune-Herald,* April 16, 2001, 1A.

29. Taylor, interview, February 25, 1999.

30. See *Annual of the Baptist General Convention of Texas* (1994), 243, and (1995), 267.

31. A. Miller, interview, January 22, 1999; Kluge, interview, January 13, 1999.

32. Anderson, interview, March 30, 1999.

33. "Springhill United Methodist Church, 133rd Homecoming"; Anderson, interview, March 30, 1999.

INTERVIEWS

Institute for Oral History, Baylor University, Waco, Texas

Anderson, Ernestine Garrett. Interviewed by Lois E. Myers, February 17 and March 30, 1999, in Riesel, Tex.

Blankenstein, Herman H. Interviewed by Lois E. Myers, April 15, 1998, in Waco, Tex.

Blankenstein, Irene Otto. Interviewed by Lois E. Myers, April 15, 1998, in Waco, Tex.

Bohne, Evelyn, and Louise Yows. Interviewed by Marla Pierson Lester, February 7, 2001, in Coryell City, Tex.

Brinkmeyer, Charles. Interviewed by Marla Pierson Lester, February 7, 2001, in Coryell City, Tex.

Bullock, Mary Ellen Nix. Interviewed by Lois E. Myers, June 27 and July 13, 1995 and February 15, 1996, in Woodway, Tex.

Chavez, Robert. Interviewed by Marla Pierson Lester, February 1, 2001, in Waco, Tex.

Dulock, Walter, Evelyn Mae Smajstrla Cunningham, Robert Cunningham, and Rosalee Smajstrla Urbis. Interviewed by Lois E. Myers, September 15, 1998, in Elk, Tex.

Duty, Wanda Coulter. Interviewed by Lois E. Myers, August 11, 1998, in Eddy, Tex.

Ellis, William Gardiner. Interviewed by Lois E. Myers, January 27, 2000, in Waco, Tex.

Evans, Cedell, and Rosena Evans. Interviewed by Jay Butler, August 26, 1993, in Post Oak community, McLennan County, Tex.

Felice, Lawrence G. Interviewed by Lois E. Myers, February 25, 1999, in Waco, Tex.

Fields, Roosevelt. Interviewed by Lois E. Myers, May 14, 1999, in Harrison, Tex.

Gallmeier, Alfred. Interviewed by Marla Pierson, December 4, 2000, in Riesel, Tex.

Garrett, Glenda Gala. Interviewed by Lois E. Myers, June 22, 1998, in Waco, Tex.

Gibson, Carol Grant. Interviewed by Lois E. Myers, February 11, 1998, in Waco, Tex.

Graves, Lonnie. Interviewed by Anne Radford Phillips, October 10, 1991, and by Jay Butler, June 30, 1993, in Satin, Tex.

Guy, Katherine. Interviewed by Jay Butler, July 28, 1993, in Satin, Tex.

Hayden, John. Interviewed by Lois E. Myers, December 10, 1998, in Riesel, Tex.

Herrington, Norma Hinze. Interviewed by Glenn Jonas, June 23, 1990, in Cego, Tex.

Herrington, Thomas, and Dorothy Herrington. Interviewed by Glenn Jonas, June 27, 1990, in Cego, Tex.

Hogan, John D., and Lynn Holt. Interviewed by Lois E. Myers, May 30, 1998, in Liberty Hill community, McLennan County, Tex.

Huber, Albert, and Flora Hildegard Hinze Huber. Interviewed by Lois E. Myers, January 20, 1999, in Belfalls, Tex.

Kluge, Lorraine Kaufman. Interviewed by Lois E. Myers, January 7 and January 13, 1999, in Waco, Tex.

Leuschner, Albert Henry. Interviewed by Lois E. Myers, February 9, 1998, in Waco, Tex.

Leuschner, Hattie Lehmann. Interviewed by Lois E. Myers, February 9, 1998, in Waco, Tex.

Long, Edna. Interviewed by Marla Pierson Lester, February 6, 2001, in Harrison, Tex.

Lovett, Jane. Interviewed by Lois E. Myers, February 12, 1998, in Woodway, Tex.

McKee, Edith Bridger. Interviewed by Glenn Jonas, June 21, 1990, in Cego, Tex.

Miller, Alice Margaret. Interviewed by Lois E. Myers, January 22, 1999, in Marlin, Tex.

Miller, Corine Niesen. Interviewed by Lois E. Myers, February 22, 1999, in Waco, Tex.

Miller, Dora Mae Hardcastle. Interviewed by Glenn Jonas, June 28, 1990, in Cego, Tex.

Miller, Helen Janet. Interviewed by Lois E. Myers, January 26, 1999, in Waco, Tex.

Richter, Donald Julius, and Wilma Marie Altus Richter. Interviewed by Lois E. Myers, September 8, 1998, in Leroy, Tex.

Rowe, Gracie Johnson. Interviewed by Lois E. Myers, July 7, 1998, in Eddy, Tex.

Rozychi, Isidore. Interviewed by Lois E. Myers, June 3, 1998, in Tours, Tex.

Schwecke, Alton H. Interviewed by Lois E. Myers, December 9, 1998, in Riesel, Tex.

Silaff, Janet Terry. Interviewed by Lois E. Myers, June 10, 1998, in Leroy, Tex.

Smith, Margaret H. Norman, and Garnet Leon Vardeman. Interviewed by Lois E. Myers, June 14, 2000, in Hewitt, Tex.

Taylor, Jeffrey W. Interviewed by Lois E. Myers, February 25, 1999, in Waco, Tex.

Trotter, Joe. Interviewed by Jay Butler, June 3, 1993, in Satin, Tex.

Tucker, Fred Douglas. Interviewed by Jay Butler, August 26, 1993, in Falls County, Tex.

Vasquez, Martin. Interviewed by Marla Pierson Lester, February 6, 2001, in Waco, Tex.

Williams, Barbara Hamilton. Interviewed by Lois E. Myers, April 21, 1998, in Waco, Tex.

Willis, Valerie London. Interviewed by Anne Radford Phillips, March 19 and April 8, 1992, in Waco, Tex.

Wittner, Lorene. Interviewed by Glenn Jonas, June 19, 1990, and February 6, 1991, in Cego, Tex.

The Texas Collection, Baylor University, Waco, Texas

Engelbrecht, Henry T. *Oral Memoirs of Henry T. Engelbrecht.* Interviewed by Ray Niederer, March 21, 1973, in Crawford, Tex.

Johnson, Eunice Brown. *Oral Memoirs of Eunice Brown Johnson.* Interviewed by Rebecca Sharpless, July 31, 1986, and April 14, 1987, in Gatesville, Tex.

Keatts, Rowena Weatherly. *Oral Memoirs of Rowena Weatherly Keatts.* Interviewed by Rebecca Sharpless, on 5 occasions from May 5, 1986 to April 15, 1987, in Waco, Tex.

Malone, Vera Estelle Allen. *Oral Memoirs of Vera Malone.* Interviewed by LaWanda Ball, December 5, 1975, in Waco, Tex.

Neal, Carl. *Oral Memoirs of Carl Neal.* Interviewed by Lois E. Myers, February 4 and February 11, 1993, in Lorena, Tex.

Oral Memoirs of Canaan Baptist Church. A series of interviews conducted by Jaclyn L. Jeffrey, Lois E. Myers, and Rebecca Sharpless from 1997 to 1998.

> Bekkelund, Ima Hoppe. Interviewed by Lois E. Myers, February 25, 1997, in Woodway, Tex.
>
> Dreyer, Edna Jaeckle. Interviewed by Lois E. Myers, May 21, 1997, in Gatesville, Tex.
>
> Engelbrecht, Benjamin Franklin. Interviewed by Rebecca Sharpless, on February 13, 1997, and (with Earlien Freyer Engelbrecht) on March 25, April 2, and April 22, 1997, in Crawford, Tex.
>
> Gauer, Jerry. Interviewed by Lois E. Myers, January 9, 1998, in Crawford, Tex.
>
> Gauer, Minnie Weber. Interviewed by Lois E. Myers, February 12, 1997, in Crawford, Tex.
>
> Massirer, Agnes Gohlke. Interviewed (with Van Doren Massirer) by Lois E. Myers, April 11, 1997, in Crawford, Tex.
>
> Massirer, Van Doren. Interviewed (with Mary Massirer) by Lois E. Myers, January 9, 1998, in Crawford, Tex.
>
> Mattlage, Marvin. Interviewed by Lois E. Myers, May 2, 1997, in Crawford, Tex.
>
> Scott, Robert Carl. Interviewed by Rebecca Sharpless, May 15, 1997, in Waco, Tex.
>
> Westerfeld, Clodius. Interviewed by Lois E. Myers, January 16, 1998, in Crawford, Tex.

Pierson, Oris E. *Oral Memoirs of Oris E. Pierson.* Interviewed by Suzanne Olsen, November 2 and 29, 1972, in Clifton, Tex.

Russell, Geneva Maxwell. *Oral Memoirs of Geneva Maxwell Russell.* Interviewed by Lois E. Myers, on 8 occasions from September 2 to November 11, 1992, in Woodway, Tex.

Simcik, Mary Hanak. *Oral Memoirs of Mary Hanak Simcik.* Interviewed by LaWanda Ball, November 24, 1975, in Waco, Tex.

Stafford, Bessie Lee Barrens. *Oral Memoirs of Bessie Lee Barrens Stafford.* Interviewed by Rebecca Sharpless, May 7, 1987, in Waco, Tex.

Weir, Bernice Porter Bostick. *Oral Memoirs of Bernice Porter Bostick Weir.* Interviewed by Rebecca Sharpless, on 4 occasions from July 9 to August 6, 1990, in Liberty Hill community, McLennan County, Tex.

Individual Church and Community Histories

"A Brief History, St. Paul United Church of Christ, Marlin, Texas." N.p. n.d. Photocopy. (located at IOH).

"Canaan Baptist Church, Crawford, Texas, 100th Anniversary, 1891–1991." N.p. 1991. Photocopy. (located at IOH).

Cunningham, Robert, Sr. *A History of the Elk Community, Texas.* N.p. 1996. (located at TXC).

Dvoracek, Mary. *Church of the Assumption, West, Texas, Centennial, 1892–1992.* West, Tex.: Czechoslovak Publishing Company, 1992. (located at TXC).

Graves, Lonnie. "Cedar Grove Baptist Church." 1986. Photocopy of typescript. (located at IOH).

Jupe, Mary Elizabeth. *A History of Tours, Texas.* San Antonio: M. E. Jupe, 1988.

Kluge, Lorraine. "History of St. Paul U.C.C." 1999. Typescript. (located at IOH).

Kuehl, Dorothy, and Karen Meyer. *Friedens Au: A Centennial History of Trinity Lutheran Church, Riesel, Texas.* Riesel, Tex.: Trinity Lutheran Church Evening Guild, 1983. (located at TXC).

Liberty Hill Baptist Church Record of Progress Committee. "Record of Progress." 1966. Typescript. (located at Liberty Hill Baptist Church, Eddy, Tex.).

Marley, Rachel M., and Evelyn Riggs Posey. *Gone but Not Forgotten: A History of Battle Cemetery and Battle Community.* [Mart, Tex.]: R. M. Marley, 1988.

Means, Bertha Sadler. *Portrait of a Pioneer in the Making, James B. Sadler, 1828–1911.* Austin: Hart Graphics, 1975.

Miller, A. A. *Evangelical Church, Cego, Texas, Sunday School Minutes, Recorded by A. A. Miller, Secretary.* N.p. 1941. Photocopy. (located at TXC).

Monroe, Renee. "The Community of South Bosque." N.p. 1977. Photocopy of typescript. (located at IOH).

"A New Church for a New World: Official Opening of Spring Hill United Methodist Church, Riesel, Texas, February 23, 1969." N.p. 1969. Photocopy. (located at IOH).

Our Savior's Lutheran Church, Norse, Texas. *Our Savior's Lutheran Church Centennial Celebration, 1869–1969.* N.p. 1969.

Perry United Methodist Church. *A Century of Methodism: Centennial Celebration June 25–July 2, 1972.* Perry, Tex.: Perry United Methodist Church, 1972.

Ringering, O. K., and Mrs. O. K. Ringering. *Canaan Baptist Church, Crawford, Texas, 75th Anniversary, Seventy-Five Years, 1891–1966.* N.p. 1966. (located at TXC).

St. Joseph's Church, Elk, Texas, Dedicated December 17, 1972. N.p. 1972.

Schack, Erna C. *Zion United Church of Christ 100th Anniversary, 1881–1981, October 25, 1981.* N.p. 1981. (located at TXC).

Schiemenz, Robert. *The First Hundred Years: A History of St. Paul's United Church of Christ, Gerald, Texas.* Waco: Central Texas Printing, 2000. (located at Waco-McLennan County Public Library, Waco, Tex.)

"75th Anniversary Celebration, October 25–26, 1975, St. Paul's United Church of Christ, Gerald, 1900–1975." N.p. 1975. Photocopy. (located at IOH).

"Southern Association Newsletter, February 2000." Austin: Southern Association of the North American Baptist Conference, 2000. (located at IOH).

"Springhill United Methodist Church, Riesel, Texas, 133rd Annual Homecoming Services, September 10, 11, 13, 1998." N.p. 1998. (located at IOH).

Souvenir Booklet Committee. *Mt. Olive Missionary Baptist Church, Downsville, Texas, 100th Year Anniversary, 1884–1994.* N.p. 1984. (located at TXC).

Souvenir of the Dedication of Saint Francis Church, on Thanksgiving Day, November 26, 1931. N.p. 1931. (located at TXC).

BOOKS, ARTICLES, AND THESES

Annual of the Baptist General Convention of Texas. Dallas: Baptist General Convention of Texas, 1990, 1994, 1995, and 1999.

Ayers, Edward L. *The Promise of the New South: Life after Reconstruction.* New York: Oxford University Press, 1992.

Baker, Clark Graham. "Photography as Document: A Study of Family Photography and Its Viability as a Truth-Telling Medium." Ph.D. dissertation, University of Alabama, 1995.

Baker, Robert A. *The Blossoming Desert: A Concise History of Texas Baptists.* Waco: Word Books, 1970.

Bedichek, Una, and George T. Baskett. *The Consolidation of Rural Schools with and without Transportation.* Bulletin of the University of Texas No. 43, General Series No. 7. Austin: University of Texas, 1904.

Berger, Michael. *The Devil Wagon in God's Country: The Automobile and Social Change in Rural America, 1893–1929.* Hamden, Conn.: Archon Books, 1979.

Bosque County History Book Committee. *Bosque County: Land and People.* Vol. 1. Dallas: Curtis Media Corporation, 1985.

Brackenridge, R. Douglas. *Voice in the Wilderness: A History of the Cumberland Presbyterian Church in Texas.* San Antonio: Trinity University Press, 1968.

Bradley, Martin B., Norman M. Green, Jr., Dale E. Jones, Mac Lynn, and Lou McNeil. *Churches and Church Membership in the United States 1990.* Atlanta: Glenmary Research Center, 1992.

Butler, Jay M. "James Harrison and the Development of Harrison Switch." Master's thesis, Baylor University, 1989.

Campbell, Randolph B. *An Empire for Slavery: The Peculiar Institution in Texas, 1821–1865.* Baton Rouge: Louisiana State University Press, 1989.

Campbell, Randolph B., and Richard G. Lowe. *Wealth and Power in Antebellum Texas.* College Station: Texas A&M University Press, 1977.

Campbell, Thomas H. *Good News on the Frontier: A History of the Cumberland Presbyterian Church*. Memphis: Frontier Press, 1960.

———. *History of the Cumberland Presbyterian Church in Texas*. Nashville: Cumberland Presbyterian Publishing House, 1936.

Cantrell, William E. "Some Advantages of School Consolidation in Bosque, Coryell, Hill, Lampasas, and McLennan Counties." Master's thesis, Southern Methodist University, 1931.

Cardoso, Lawrence A. *Mexican Emigration to the United States 1897–1931: Socio-Economic Patterns*. Tucson: University of Arizona Press, 1980.

Carroll, J. M. *A History of Texas Baptists*. Edited by J. B. Cranfill. Dallas: Baptist Standard Publishing Co., 1923.

———. *Texas Baptist Statistics, 1895*. Houston: J. J. Pastoriza Printing and Litho. Co., 1895. Centennial edition reprint. Dallas: Texas Baptist Historical Committee, Baptist General Convention of Texas, 1985.

Castañeda, Carlos E. *The Church in Texas since Independence, 1836–1950*. Vol. 7, *Our Catholic Heritage in Texas*. New York: Arno Press, 1976.

Clark, Thomas D. *Pills, Petticoats, and Plows: The Southern Country Store*. Norman: University of Oklahoma Press, 1989.

Dolan, Jay P. "The Immigrants and Their Gods: A New Perspective in American Religious History." In *American Church History: A Reader,* ed. Henry Warner Bowden and P. C. Kemeny, 60–71. Nashville: Abingdon Press, 1998.

Dudley, Carl S. *Where Have All Our People Gone? New Choices for Old Churches*. New York: The Pilgrim Press, 1979.

Dunn, David, Paul N. Crusius, Josias Friedli, Theophil W. Menzel, Carl E. Schneider, William Toth, and James E. Wagner. *A History of the Evangelical and Reformed Church*. Reprint of 1961 edition, with introduction by Lowell H. Zuck. New York: The Pilgrim Press, 1990.

DuPuy, Louisa Romans. "Social Trends in McLennan County, Texas." Master's thesis, Baylor University, 1934.

Elam, Richard. "Baptist Ministers and Slavery in Antebellum Texas." *Texas Baptist History* 9 (1989): 1–11.

Ellison, Ronald C. *Texas and Baptist Sunday Schools, 1829–1996*. Dallas: Baptist General Convention of Texas, 1997.

Fite, Gilbert. *Cotton Fields No More: Southern Agriculture 1865–1980*. Lexington: University Press of Kentucky, 1984.

Grindal, Bruce T. "The Religious Interpretation of Experience in a Black Community." In *Holding on to the Land and the Lord: Kinship, Ritual, Land Tenure, and Social Policy in the Rural South,* ed. Robert L. Hall and Carol B. Stack, 89–101. Athens: University of Georgia Press, 1982.

Harsch, Lloyd. "Baptist Witness among Germans in Texas." *Texas Baptist History* 17 (1997): 89–123.

Hill, Samuel S., ed. *Encyclopedia of Religion in the South*. Macon, Ga.: Mercer University Press, 1984.

Jackson, John Brinkerhoff. *A Sense of Place, A Sense of Time*. New Haven: Yale University Press, 1994.

Jordan, Terry G., with John L. Bean, Jr., and William M. Holmes. *Texas: A Geography*. Boulder, Colo.: Westview Press, 1984.

Kelley, Dayton, ed. *The Handbook of Waco and McLennan County, Texas*. Waco: Texian Press, 1972.

Koenig, Robert J. *Pause to Ponder: A History of the Lutheran Church-Missouri Synod of Texas*. N.p.: Texas District The Lutheran Church-Missouri Synod, 1980.

Loud, I. B. "Methodism and the Negroes." In *History of Texas Methodism 1900–1960,* ed. Olin W. Nail, 87–112. Austin: Capital Printing Company, 1961.

McBeth, Harry Leon. *Texas Baptists: A Sesquicentennial History*. Dallas: Baptistway Press, 1998.

McWilliams, Carey. *North from Mexico: The Spanish-Speaking People of the United States.* New York: Greenwood Press, 1968.

Meinig, D. W. *Imperial Texas: An Interpretive Essay in Cultural Geography*. Austin: University of Texas Press, 1969.

Montgomery, William E. "The Formation of African American Churches." Introduction to *Black Churches in Texas: A Guide to Historic Congregations,* by Clyde McQueen, 3–22. College Station: Texas A&M University Press, 2000.

———. *Under Their Own Vine and Fig Tree: The African-American Church in the South, 1865–1900.* Baton Rouge: Louisiana State University Press, 1993.

Phelan, Macum. *A History of Early Methodism in Texas, 1817–1866.* Nashville: Cokesbury Press, 1924.

Pierson, Oris Emerald. "Norwegian Settlements in Bosque County, Texas." Master's thesis, University of Texas, 1947.

Poage, W. R. *McLennan County—Before 1980.* Waco: Texian Press, 1981.

Radford, Garry H., Sr. *African American Heritage in Waco, Texas.* Austin: Eakin Press, 2000.

Schlereth, Thomas J. *Victorian America: Transformations in Everyday Life, 1876–1915.* New York: HarperCollins, 1991.

Sharpless, Rebecca. "Fertile Ground, Narrow Choices: Women on Cotton Farms of the Texas Blackland Prairie, 1900–1940." Ph.D. dissertation, Emory University, 1993.

———. *Fertile Ground, Narrow Choices: Women on Texas Cotton Farms, 1900–1940.* Chapel Hill: University of North Carolina Press, 1999.

Shover, John L. *First Majority, Last Minority: The Transforming of Rural Life in America.* DeKalb: Northern Illinois University Press, 1976.

Starr, Sarah Joyce Rutherford. "'Yours Heart and Hand': An Analysis of the Correspondence of James and Patience Crain Black, 1861–1865." Master's thesis, Baylor University, 1990.

Svrcek, V. A., trans. and ed. *A History of the Czech-Moravian Catholic Communities of Texas.* Waco: Texian Press, 1974.

Texas Almanac, 1992–1993. Dallas Morning News, 1991.

———, *2000–2001. Dallas Morning News,* 1999.

Tyler, Ron, Douglas E. Barnett, Roy R. Barkley, Penelope C. Anderson, and Mark F. Odintz, eds. *The New Handbook of Texas.* Austin: The Texas State Historical Association, 1996.

United Church of Christ. *Year Book of the United Church of Christ.* New York: The United Church of Christ, 1968.

Vernon, Walter N., Robert W. Sledge, Robert C. Monk, and Norman W. Spellman. *The Methodist Excitement in Texas: A History.* Dallas: The Texas United Methodist Historical Society, 1984.

Walker, J. L., and C. P. Lumpkin. *History of the Waco Baptist Association of Texas.* Waco: Byrne-Hill Printing House, 1897.

Williams, Charles. "The Conversion Ritual in a Rural Black Baptist Church." In *Holding on to the Land and the Lord: Kinship, Ritual, Land Tenure, and Social Policy in the Rural South,* ed. Robert L. Hall and Carol B. Stack, 69–79. Athens: University of Georgia Press, 1982.

GOVERNMENT DOCUMENTS

McLennan County. Deed Records. Waco, Tex.

——. Probate Records. Waco, Tex.

National Archives and Records Services. Population Schedules of the Eighth Census of the United States, 1860, Texas. Slave Schedules. Washington, D.C.: National Archives, 1967. Microfilm.

U.S. Department of Agriculture. *1997 Census of Agriculture.* Available online from http://www.nass.usda.gov/census.

U.S. Department of Commerce, Bureau of the Census. *Fifteenth Census of the United States.* Vol. 3, Part 2, *Population.* Washington, D.C.: Government Printing Office, 1932.

NEWSPAPERS

Baptist Standard, 1998, 2001.

McGregor Mirror, 1977.

Waco Tribune-Herald, 1978, 1987, 1990, 1997, 2000, 2001.

ONLINE INTERNET SOURCES

Biblical Witness Fellowship. *Biblical Witness Fellowship: Renewing the United Church of Christ.* Available from http://biblicalwitness.org/

Inter-University Consortium for Political and Social Research. *Historical United States Census Data Browser.* Available from http://fisher.lib.virginia.edu/census.

Library of Congress American Memory Collection. *American Life Histories: Manuscripts from the Federal Writers' Project, 1936–1940.* Available from http://memory.loc.gov/ammem/wpaintro/wpahome.html.

Texas Historical Commission. *Texas Historic Sites Atlas.* Available from http://atlas.thc.state.tx.us.

United Church of Christ. *United Church of Christ.* Available from http://www.ucc.org.

Unity of the Brethren. *Unity of the Brethren.* Available from http://www.unityofthebrethren.org.

INDEX